DESIGNING HOMES

for

People with Dementia

Damian Utton BA(Hons) DipArch RIBA

PUBLISHED BY *The Journal of Dementia Care*

First published in 2007 by
Journal of Dementia Care
Hawker Publications
Culvert House
Culvert Road
London SW11 5DH
Tel 020 7720 2108
Fax 020 7498 3023
Email suec@hawkerpublications.com
Web www.careinfo.org

British Library Cataloguing in Publication Data

A catalogue record for this book is available from the British Library

ISBN-10: 1 874790 28 0
ISBN-13: 978 1874790 28 0

Design by Andrew Chapman (design@awrc.info)

Printed and bound in Great Britain by
Hastings Printing Company, St Leonards-on-Sea, East Sussex

The Journal of Dementia Care
The Journal of Dementia Care is published six times a year and is recognised as the leading specialist journal on dementia care.
For subscription enquiries please contact Esco Business Services, 01371 851802.

Also from Hawker Publications:
Design for Dementia, edited by Stephen Judd, Mary Marshall and Peter Phippen.
ISBN 1 874790 35 3

Contents

Introduction

About the author

Damian Utton BA(Hons) DipArch RIBA is a chartered architect at Pozzoni Design Group, where he is an Associate. Pozzoni Design Group an architectural practice based in Altrincham, near Manchester, UK. (www.pozzoni-group.co.uk)

The 17 years' experience gained since professional qualification has been largely spent working in the social housing and special needs sector and this has progressed to the design of sheltered housing for the elderly and specialised care homes.

A six-month sabbatical during 2005 provided the opportunity to travel and gain further knowledge of care home design around the world. This publication has come about as a result of this study-tour.

Other interests include competitive athletics, travelling and supporting Southampton Football Club.

The history of this book

In 2005 my employers, Pozzoni Design Group, kindly allowed me to take a six-month sabbatical from architectural practice in order to develop my interest in the design of accommodation for people with dementia. This arose from several commissions for buildings for people with dementia in the UK. Since I also had a passion for travel, I thought I would use the six months to travel all over the world visiting buildings for people with dementia and to share the knowledge I acquired: hence this book.

I visited 72 homes in nine countries between April and October 2005 and editing this down to the 25 presented in this book has not been an easy task. The buildings chosen illustrate points of interest, which in my view can inform, and hopefully improve, the design of future facilities. I have also attempted to show homes which represent what I found to be current dementia design.

I took the view that design for dementia is helpful for everybody since we all benefit from more understandable buildings, especially if we are confused for some reason such as tiredness or stress. Any building for older people, even those currently without dementia, should be dementia-friendly since it then offers a greater flexibility should there be future changes in the profile of people who live there.

This publication does not attempt to differentiate between the nature of the facilities featured or to compare one unit with another. Each country has a different system, social policies, regulations, funding and nomenclature which have a direct influence on the design and layout. Such constraints and parameters are constantly changing with distinctions and boundaries becoming increasingly blurred. For example, the term "housing with support" in the UK would be similar to "hostels" or "low care" in Australia, "assisted living" in the USA and to some extent "group living" in Scandinavia.

Approaches to dementia

The Dementia Services Development Centre at the University of Stirling suggests three approaches to understanding dementia and that all three approaches should be considered when developing any form of service. The aim should be to optimise all three models. They are:

The Medical Model which is concerned with diagnosis and treatment. A differential diagnosis between the main forms of dementia: Alzheimer's disease, vascular dementia and Lewy body dementia is important. Treating concomitant physical and psychiatric ailments is a focus of attention since there are limited drugs available for dementia. The role of design is to enable people with dementia to be well looked after and safe.

The Disability Model suggests that the experience of dementia has multiple causes since the person with dementia has to relate to their social and built environment which may be helpful or may exacerbate their disability. As far as design is concerned, people have impairments; disability is caused by the failure of design to compensate for them.

The Citizenship Model takes the view that people with dementia have a lot to contribute to society and have rights and responsibilities. Design should celebrate their creativity and provide opportunities for helping and giving. People with dementia should be involved in the design process with their views taken into account. Space should be provided for creative activity to take place and to display the results.

Most people with dementia are older people and the interaction of dementia with the other impairments of old age such as impaired mobility, vision and hearing should also be considered.

Design for dementia

Leading on from the three approaches, Mary Marshall (1998) summarises the impairments of dementia as:

• Impaired memory
• Impaired reasoning
• Impaired ability to learn
• High level of stress
• Acute sensitivity to the social and the built environment.

In the same publication she summarises the international consensus on design principles as:

• Design should compensate for impairments
• Design should maximise independence
• Design should enhance self esteem and confidence
• Design should demonstrate care for staff
• Design should be orientating and understandable
• Design should reinforce personal identity
• Design should welcome relatives and the local community
• Design should allow the control of stimuli.

Applying the approaches and the principles to practice

Following on from the three approaches and the principles above, the way it works in practice can be explained in more detail.

Impaired memory can be compensated for by creating high levels of visibility across an open plan area and avoiding corridors wherever possible or having them as short and wide as possible with an 'event' at the end so there are no dead-ends. Toilet doors should always be visible with the toilet in the en-suite visible from the bed. Lots of visual information and light is essential. Dementia usually affects recent memory most so design should be familiar to a time when a person's memory is at its best. Cultural considerations are an important factor and people's homes as young adults will have varied greatly in terms of urban/rural, income, country of origin and so on.

Impaired reasoning can mean that people with dementia cannot understand their own impairments. They will, for example, not understand that they can no longer perceive three dimensions and will fail to understand stairs or contrasting colour in flooring which they may see as a step. The implications of this are that stairs should have very clear nosings and a clear skirting board to reinforce the fact that they go down and up. Different types of flooring need to be of the same tone to avoid the person seeing a step.

I need to digress here to mention the much-misunderstood issue of colour perception. As they get older most people lose the ability to differentiate between colours, so colour contrast rather than colours is the key to orientation. The ability to discriminate between colours fails first at the violet end of the spectrum with the red/orange/yellow end failing last, so these latter colours may be more effective for some people. Colours can of course be useful to assist younger relatives and staff to find their way, but usually not the people with dementia. I have included colour for orientation in some of the descriptions of units because it was mentioned to me, however in each case it could well have worked because of colour contrast rather than the actual colour. Wall junctions will be more easily perceived, for example, if the two walls are of contrasting colours, or a colour and a neutral tone.

I mentioned that older people can have a range of sight impairments. People with dementia will not understand that they have an impairment so will not be able to work out what they are seeing. Strong visual and tactile cues in handrails will help although people may not be able to work out why there is a knob on the end of a handrail. It may nevertheless make them stop at a door.

Compensating for impaired learning requires good signage and multiple cues since people with dementia will not be able to learn how to find their way. Over time they may be able to learn simple features which is why it is important to be consistent. Making all toilet doors the same colour which contrasts with the wall and the same eye-level sign with words and a picture will help. Objects are better than colour for orientation; a curved wall, a wall hanging or a plant for example. A kitchen being visible from all communal areas of a household will help a resident find their way. Staff doors should be hidden to avoid the frustration of people trying to open a locked door. Blending these doors into the surrounding wall finish can successfully achieve this.

Credits

I am very grateful to everyone I met between April and October 2005 for their help, kindness and hospitality. This book would not have been possible without the incredible generosity of all the people who took time out of their own busy schedules to help me. A special thank you to Professor Mary Marshall for her guidance and support throughout this project. So many people have contributed to the production of this book that I cannot list everyone by name – but a big thank you to each and every one of you!

High levels of stress can be a consequence of the frustration that can arise from a person's impairments and the failure of design to compensate for these. Small numbers of people in a household allow for a family lifestyle which can be less stressful than living in a larger group of people, who could be perceived as strangers. This is an issue that often requires compromise due to costs, staffing levels and funding regimes. Providing alternate spaces such as alcoves and quiet lounges reduces stress levels not only in the people with dementia but with their families and the people that provide care for them. In my visits I found that most residents like to be where the action is but a few liked a quiet place.

An increased dependence on the senses is an obvious corollary of diminishing intellectual ability. Care should be taken to ensure that the sensory input is positive. Glare may hurt the ageing eye and needs to be avoided. Reflections and dark shadows should be avoided since light reflecting on a polished floor can be perceived as water. The use of touch, smell and sound should be emphasised but with great care to avoid sensory overload. A kitchen opening out on to a lounge area allows the smell and sounds of food being prepared to stimulate a person's senses and provide cues about mealtimes and eating. Many people lose the ability to differentiate sounds as they get older; people with dementia do not understand that they have this impairment and can be overwhelmed by too much noise.

Many people with dementia like to walk a lot and may not be able to explain why. It may be a lifetime habit, it may be a consequence of stress or it may result from pain and so on (see Marshall and Allan 2006). Design should provide opportunities for walking inside or outside, depending on the weather, and at the same time allow unobtrusive observation by staff and families. Hiding non-accessible doors and gates and making fences inconspicuous will ensure that people with dementia are not alerted to opportunities to leave the premises, as will distractions like benches and things to look at along the way.

Design should enhance self-esteem and confidence by allowing people to maintain skills they may have used in the past. This can range from peeling vegetables to playing a musical instrument. Providing people with an opportunity to make a contribution is also essential. Setting a table, helping with meal preparation, clearing up, folding laundry: all can contribute to the daily life of any household and design should allow for this to happen.

Design should demonstrate care for staff by having good staff facilities, meeting rooms, training spaces, an office away from the residential area, adequate storage and avoiding long distances for staff to travel over the course of a typical shift. There should also be a space where staff can get away from it all to help them cope with stressful situations that may arise.

Design should reinforce the personal identity of the people who live there. Cultural backgrounds should be considered. Providing space for personal possessions and furniture and allowing the opportunity for room doors to be personalised or providing a display cabinet by the door can all be helpful.

Design should welcome residents and the local community with a generally domestic, non-institutional feel, a welcoming entrance and the opportunity to do ordinary things. The design should allow, as far as possible, for people to continue with their daily life and activities as if they were still living in their own home. Residents should be able to relate to the size, scale and ambience of the spaces as a continuation of the domestic spaces they have grown up with, be it a suburban house of a city apartment block.

Design should allow for control of stimuli. Uncontrolled stimulation of the senses can be overwhelming for the person with dementia. The ability to keep noise down by use of sound-absorbing materials and finishes, blinds/curtains to control bright sunlight and good, natural and mechanical ventilation all help to minimise and control external stimuli. Open-plan kitchens allow cooking smells to permeate around and provide stimulation.

Some designers would rather work to a checklist and I have provided one in the appendix. A checklist cannot, of course, cover every aspect of a building and it is important that the impairments of old age and dementia are fully understood and the principles applied to any design.

The way this book is organised

The 25 case studies illustrate how design can compensate for some of the impairments of old age and dementia. Each building was built in accordance with the principles of care of the provider which I have listed. They comply in every case with the principles listed earlier in this introduction. The case studies are listed in alphabetical order.

For each case study there is a page of basic information, plus reasons why it has been included. The philosophy of care is listed, along with the provider's view of how this is carried through to the design of the building. *Where I am quoting the provider or paraphrasing their views, I have put the text in italics*. I asked each provider what aspects of the building they felt were worth repeating and this is then listed along with any other comments they made about it. Each case study concludes with my own comments. On the whole these are positive but **occasionally I draw attention to features I think are problematic, and I have highlighted these points in blue**. I photographed key features of each case study (with one exception, Denville Hall, where some of the photographs were taken by David Wrightson) and the captions mainly draw attention to the positive features. **Again, features I think are problematic are highlighted in blue**.

This publication is not intended to be prescriptive nor an academic dissertation. It follows a very successful book of case studies published by the *Journal of Dementia Care* in 1998 (Judd *et al*). It is clear that there is an audience of people in dementia care who find it useful to learn how others all over the world are meeting the challenges of designing for people with dementia. It is my aim to show examples of current good practice, and how the built environment facilitates and encourages the provision of care and improves the quality of life for residents, their families and staff.

A client's perspective

Nick Dykes BA(Hons), MBA, RMN
Chief Executive
CLS Care Services Ltd

The current situation

How each individual responds to the effects of dementia varies widely. Like any disability the resources available to the individual with dementia significantly affect how they cope. When I say resources I include the help available from family, friends, local services, personal income and assets and the individual's own personal attributes.

The job of the 'social services', to use a generic term, is to increase and expand the personal resources available.

Care homes in particular can help people overcome the effects of their dementia, or conversely they can actually magnify the effects.

A poorly-designed or poorly-run care home increases confusion and disorientation, obstructs patterns of communication and damages the fragile confidence of people with dementia. Sadly this situation is all too common. Many of the care homes currently operating in the UK were never designed with the needs of people with dementia in mind. The buildings and the way the staff teams work actually add to the disability of dementia.

My colleagues and I have seen this situation in our own homes in the north-west of England. We operate former local authority stock built in the 1960s and designed for a population that was able to manage their own daily living needs with some assistance. The people for whom these homes were built now manage perfectly well in their own homes with domiciliary care and, increasingly, telecare assistance.

Since the advent of community care in the early 1990s the use of care homes has been rationed to those in greatest need, and they now serve a function that was previously assigned to the health services. Back in the 60s and 70s people with dementia would find themselves in psychogeriatric wards in the local psychiatric hospital where they would live an institutional existence. Happily these places are now gone but they are yet to be replaced, for many people with dementia at least, with a more satisfactory solution. Our old care homes are little more than a stop-gap solution.

Increasing need

Currently around 750,000 people in the UK have dementia. The Alzheimer's Society predicts a steady growth to 870,000 people in 2010 and 1.8million by 2050.

More than 97% of people with dementia are over the age of 65 and it is said that one in five people aged over 80 have dementia (www.alzheimers.org.uk).

With this as a background the provision of services for people with dementia is a major issue for social carers in the public, private and voluntary sectors.

The government in England has set exacting targets for local authorities to ensure that older people can remain independent in their own homes for as long as possible. Resources have moved, over the years, from the care home sector towards 'home care' solutions.

Now a hybrid solution is on offer through the advent, and heavy promotion by government, of 'extra-care housing'. This service goes one or more steps further than 'sheltered housing' by providing ready-made communities, on-site care teams and environments designed to cope and adapt with increasing levels of physical disability. These schemes provide a self-contained flat for each occupant and offer shared facilities, such as restaurant, laundry and residents' lounge elsewhere in the complex. Opinion is polarised on whether extra-care can take over from care homes as the dominant form of provision.

The design of new care homes specifically for people with dementia has been slow to catch on. The work of the late Professor Tom Kitwood at Bradford University in the 1990s prompted some organisations, notably Methodist Homes for the Aged, to commission new designs based on the principles that Professor Kitwood described. These new care homes are still few and far between.

I predict that the need for new care homes for people with dementia will be a hot topic in the next five to 10 years. By this time much of the existing care home stock will have disappeared and those existing homes that survive will be the ones which were designed principally as nursing homes with facilities to care for people who are physically frail rather than for people with dementia.

The care home of the future

Living out one's life in a care home is for most of us an unwanted destination. Many, many older people will express a wish to 'not end up in a care home'. The reality though is that for many people the disability of dementia will eventually mean that living 'at home' is just not viable.

The move to a care home often follows bereavement or a health crisis. Often the family carers find they can no longer cope and reluctantly seek the services of a care home for regular short breaks or for a permanent move.

The need for supported care home services for people with dementia is not going to diminish, it will almost certainly increase but it must improve and cater very specifically for their needs.

A care home that serves people with dementia should provide:

- **A homelike environment** – where those providing the care and those receiving it can live alongside each other and share activities rather like a family would
- **An environment that allows individuals to be themselves** – where independence and individuality is prized and enhanced
- **A sense of ease** – where each resident can master their surroundings and feel comfortable in them

So often our buildings hinder or even prevent us from doing these seemingly simple things. How do you foster 'a sense of ease' in a hotel-like corridor of endless bedrooms, a canteen-like dining room and a lounge full of identical winged chairs?

My colleagues have experimented in recent years by converting wings of existing care homes to provide small 'dementia-friendly units' providing for no more than 10 residents. We have knocked down walls, experimented with colour contrast and fitted a domestic-scale kitchen. Generally we have made the environment 'homelike'. We intend that these units are a precursor of new homes that we plan to build and we hope to learn from the experience of operating them.

The results have been dramatic. Staff members began to behave differently. They forgot about their 'daily tasks' and instead started to think about what the individual residents wanted and needed. They gave up their meal breaks and instead sat down with residents to share meals. They threw away their institutional uniforms and began wearing their own clothes.

The knock-on effect has been that residents have been less confused, less agitated, more able to do things for themselves. Previously we relied on key-pads fitted to the entrance doors to keep residents safe from wandering. These key-pads are also fitted to the converted wings but have since become largely redundant as residents are more settled and are no longer searching for the way home.

I offer this as a simple justification for good design. The way the environment is designed has a profound effect on the way the space is used.

Wohnanlage 'Auf der Aue'

WOHNANLAGE 'AUF DER AUE'
Phillipsruher Allee 14
Hanau
Germany

Contact for further information
info@mls-hanau.de

Owner Martin Luther Foundation

Website www.mls-hanau.de

Street Elevation: The households for the people with dementia are located on the upper floors, with the roof terrace to the left-hand side of the photograph. Communal areas for the whole development are located on the ground floor, including a café opening onto a shaded terraced area. The whole development is built on a plinth, allowing servicing below and the buildings to be above the noise of the busy road.

Open since
September 2003

Resident profile
18 residents with dementia in the main building. The first floor is for people with severe dementia, second floor for people with moderate dementia. There are three and four storey blocks of sheltered housing on the rest of the site containing a total of 79 dwellings.

Number of residents
Two households of nine residents: 18 residents total.

Typical bedroom floor area
Varies from 18.7sq.m to 21.4sq.m

Floor area of each household
855sq.m

Building density
95sq.m/resident

Site area
2140sq.m (not including sheltered housing blocks or gardens)

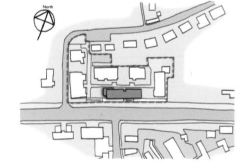

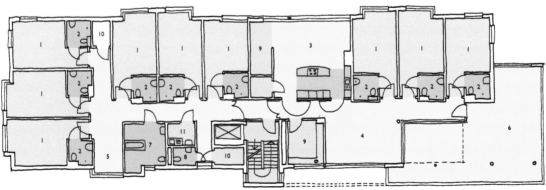

1. Bedroom x 9
2. Ensuite
3. Kitchen/Dining
4. Lounge
5. Sitting Alcove
6. Roof Terrace
7. Assisted Bathroom
8. WC
9. Staff
10. Store
11. Sluice

Site density
18sq.m/resident (not including sheltered housing blocks or gardens)

Staffing
Unknown

Service and ancillary space
The ground floor and basement of the main block contains facilities for all the sheltered housing residents and those with dementia. These include a café, library, multi-purpose room, physiotherapy, gymnasium with sauna and health suite as well as offices and administration, plant room, car parking and storage.

The staff base to each household is an alcove located off the dining area. There is also a separate utility/staff room and sluice room for each household.

Meals and laundry
There is an open plan kitchen/dining area for each household.

Site context
Inner-city urban site on a busy road close to the city centre.

Philosophy of care
The Martin Luther Foundation aims to provide "as much assistance as necessary, as much independence as possible". This means:
* *Live and work on the basis of providing the best care for older people*
* *Act and plan creatively and innovatively*
* *Develop and practise new tasks and methods.*

Philosophy expression in the building design
* *Households of nine residents allow for closer attention from staff.*
* *Variety of spaces allows residents to make their own choices where they would like to be.*
* *Roof terrace allows residents to watch the world and everyday life going by outside.*

Aspects of the building design that work well and are which are worth repeating
* *Raising whole site on a plinth above noise and fumes of traffic.*
* *Large outdoor roof terrace is popular and screen to the road reduces noise.*
* *The kitchen island allows staff to face residents when working in the kitchen and not to turn their back on people.*

Other comments
* *The lounge area is little used in comparison to the kitchen/dining area.*
* *There have been no reported problems with the residents with dementia and the roof terrace.*

Kitchen/Dining (above): The cooking area faces into the room so staff do not have to turn their back on residents. The projection on the worktop avoids the danger of accidentally touching the hob when leaning on the worktop.

Bedroom doors: personalised effect added by staff and residents, **not built in**.

Bedroom corridor: Glare from windows and a shiny floor surface could be perceived as being **wet**. This corridor feels more like a 'hotel' or apartment block corridor than a house.

Ensuite: Poor contrast between sanitary ware and rails and wall tiling. Skirting board tile and flooring has the same dark tone which could be problematic – this bottom tile may be perceived as part of the floor. The tap to the wash-basin is not traditional-looking.

AUTHOR'S COMMENT

This building is a clean, crisp modern design on an inner-city site and provides an urban style of living for people with dementia. The layout and appearance is of an apartment block or hotel. For people who lived all their lives in city apartment blocks this can be a more familiar environment than a suburban or rural house.

The kitchen/dining area is the focus of each household and residents appear to prefer to spend their time here during the day as this is where most of the activity is. The kitchen island faces into the room so staff working there do not have their back to the residents. The worksurface bows out in front of the hotplate to reduce the risk of someone accidentally resting their hand on a hot surface. There are two doors into the kitchen/dining which can open back 180degrees against the wall, allowing direct views from the staircase to the lounge area and the household front door. Dining room furniture is modern, in contrast to lounge and alcove which have more traditional furniture.

The staff base is an alcove of the dining area is barrier-free and can be used as a quiet corner if needed.

The lounge area is open-plan and well-proportioned with much daylight. As with many other homes that have a kitchen/dining area, the lounge is used only as a quiet or TV area as activity is associated with the kitchen.

Internal finishes are neutral. Vinyl flooring throughout is softened by the use of rugs, plain painted walls and ceilings and there are simple timber handrails, pictures, wall mounted lights and veneer doors.

A corridor runs along the building linking the central entrance door to the common areas and bedrooms. One end finishes in a seating alcove and the other end opens out to the roof terrace so there are 'events' and no dead-ends.

The roof terrace has a slatted screen from the main road to reduce noise and pollution and is open to the inside of the site and the sheltered housing blocks. Solid guarding and planting boxes help keep residents away from the perimeter and reduce the risk of climbing over. The second floor roof terrace is cut away to allow daylight to the terrace and lounge below.

Roof terrace with cut-out to allow daylight to floor below. Lounge is behind windows.

Because all the bedroom doors look the ◄ same, some residents have fixed their own items to the doors to help with recognition. Rugs are a potential trip hazard and in some countries would not be permitted.

The bedrooms are well-sized with large windows. Residents can bring their own furniture but the bed is provided.

The bedrooms have either two windows or a projecting bay with a small window to the short side of the bay. Thus there are two views available from each bedroom. Window cills are low and the windows are bottom-hung with an external rail for safety. There are also external

Bedroom: Bed is provided but residents' own furniture otherwise.

blinds which control solar gain better than internal blinds. Both these items are designed into the building façade. Conventional curtains internally create a more domestic appearance. Residents' own furniture (apart from the bed) are usually traditional in appearance and sits within the neutral background.

The ground floor of the block has communal facilities for the whole site. This building is raised up on a plinth above the level of the street traffic and access is via steps and ramp to the front door or an open garden area. All ground floor windows look out over the traffic to the other side of the busy road. The plinth also allows for servicing to be underneath the building.

A café to one side of the entrance reception opens out to the garden area and this acts as a social hub for the whole site. Families and visitors can also use this facility. There is also a library, multi-purpose room, physiotherapy and health centre with gymnasium, sauna, steam room, etc. Offices and administration are also located on the ground floor. By locating all these common facilities here the sheltered housing residents, visitors, families and the community are brought into the building where the people with dementia live, breaking down any barriers or stigma that may arise from having residents with dementia in a separate building.

Urban and brownfield sites are becoming more common for development as elderly persons' residential accommodation. This building is a good example of how to address the issues arising from such sites in conjunction with dementia design issues.

➤ **The en-suite door does not face into the room itself which frees up wall space but does not allow a view of the wc. The en-suite lacks contrast with white tiling, white sanitary ware and white grabrails and has a clinical appearance.**

Lounge: Rugs soften the appearance of the vinyl flooring. Traditional furniture contrasts with a very contemporary building. **Current UK practice would not allow this because of a potential trip hazard. There is a strong contrast between rug and floor which could also be perceived as a step.**

Birralee

REASONS FOR SELECTION
➤ **Different floor layouts for different households**
➤ **Use of cueing for orientation**
➤ **Village square concept**
➤ **Extensive garden areas**
➤ **Residents' freedom of movement between households**

BIRRALEE
Birralee Nursing Home
155 Odin Road
Innaloo
Western Australia
Australia

Contact for further information
welcome@brightwatergroup.com

Owner Brightwater Care Group

Website www.brightwatergroup.com

Village Square: Community building is to the left, office building with turret roof and the service entry is behind. On special occasions this is used for parties and as a village square for the community within the development. A clock tower above the service entry (not shown) also acts as a landmark.

Open since
1998

Architect
Brian J. Kidd in association with Kidd and Povey, Perth

Resident profile
Birralee is not a secure site so there are no actively mobile residents with dementia.

Number of residents
Four households of 15 residents: 60 residents total.
One of the households is for Russian Orthodox residents, mostly of Serbian, Russian and Macedonian origin. Staff from these backgrounds are also employed here.

Typical bedroom floor area
19.5sq.m plus 6.0sq.m ensuite: 25.5sq.m total.

Floor area of each household
Linear households: 697sq.m
'Y'-shape households: 780sq.m

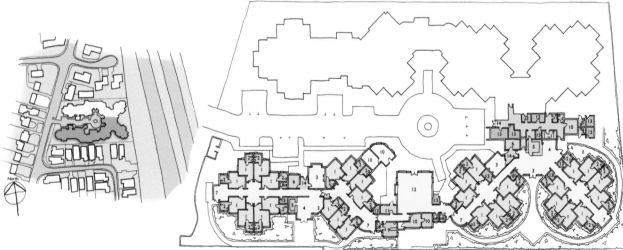

1. Bedroom
2. Ensuite
3. Lounge
4. Dining
5. Kitchen
6. Study/staff base
7. Alcove
8. WC
9. Assisted bathroc
10. Office/admin
11. Utility room
12. Club room
13. Store
14. Entrance

Building density

Linear households: 46sq.m per resident
'Y'-shaped households: 52sq.m per resident

Site area

8052sq.m

Site density

134.2sq.m per resident

Staffing

There is one care manager and one clinical nurse.
Care staff during the day are:
Morning: two registered nurses, one enrolled nurse, nine care staff and three ancillary staff.
Afternoon: two registered nurses, eight care staff and two ancillary staff.
Overnight: one registered nurse and three care staff.

Service and ancillary space

Each household has its own kitchen. Utility rooms are spread throughout the building. There is a central service core to the rear of the site which services two of the households directly; the other two households are service via external access or through one of the other households.
Deliveries are via the central driveway.

Meals and laundry

The kitchen of each household is for drinks and snacks and reheating food only. All meals are prepared off-site on a cook-chill basis. Relatives are free to use the kitchen at any time. Laundry is contracted out but there are three utility rooms located between the households.

Site context

Flat suburban site in Perth. A busy highway passes behind the site.

Philosophy of care

Brightwater Care Group statement of purpose is:
• *To enable well-being*
• *Values: people, caring, learning, innovation*
• *Philosophy: Personhood*
• *Quality statement: quality of care and services means achieving satisfaction for all (our) customers. Brightwater Care Group is committed to this concept, with every member of every team in the organisation empowered to contribute to the continuous improvement process.*

View from kitchen showing views to bedroom corridor and alcove to the 'Y' shaped household: General clutter, as found in any home, gives a lived-in homely feel. Residents can see their way around the household from here as well as staff being able to monitor residents discreetly.

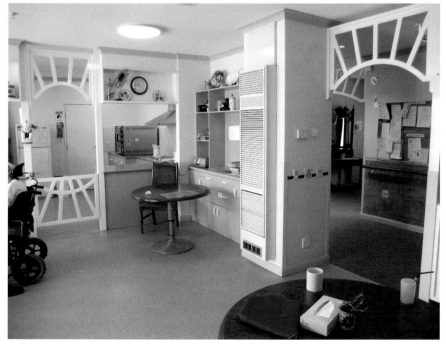

Kitchen/Dining: Each household has different motifs and colour schemes (see introduction) to identify each household and for residents to orientate themselves around the whole building. Cabinets allow for displays which are changed on a regular basis. Kitchen gate can be closed if a potentially hazardous activity is taking place in the kitchen e.g. floor just been cleaned and is slippery. **Change in floor contrast between kitchen and hallway could be perceived as a step by people with dementia.** The opening also allows for view of the entrance hall.

Bedroom: Coloured skirting boards and architraves help to identify each room (see introduction) and these contrast with walls behind making the wall/floor junction clear and outlining the en-suite door. Small window also provides views outside from the bed.

Additionally, all Brightwater services reflect the concept of personhood and a person-centred approach forms the umbrella theory under which all management, people services, training, care practices and support services will operate."

Philosophy expression in the building design
A domestic homelike environment allows the person-centred care approach to be realised. Residents are free to walk between the households and ease of access allows staff to support each other in delivering care.

Each household has its own personality and identity.

Aspects of the building design that work well and which are worth repeating?
The different themes of colour and motifs in each household work well to orientate residents and staff to their location, as do the two different types of layout plan.

The communal gardens are successful and provide variety and sun/shade for all throughout the day.

The village square is a success, acting as a focal point for the whole scheme. This space is used as such, for street parties and other events.

Front doors for each household allow families to visit without going via a central reception area, which can be perceived as institutional.

Rear gardens: Pergolas provide shading and there is a wide variety of colours and textures

Other comments
Visitors and families often comment on the friendly atmosphere.
Good team spirit enables residents and staff wellbeing.

AUTHOR'S COMMENT
There are many aspects of the building which make this project a success.

The village square, with the office block as a separate building, the clubhouse, fountain and deliveries porch with weather vane, become the central focus of the scheme. This space is used for parties and similar events, as a real village square would be.

There is not a separate delivery entrance, so all goods in and out come through the drive and the village square. This would happen in a normal street, where car parking, refuse collection, postman, etc. are all part of daily life.

Veranda and pathway from sitting area at end of corridor: All pathways lead back into the building so there are no dead ends. Border on paths helps to define the edge of walking areas, useful for people with visual impairments.

The design of this village square and delivery access creates a 'normal' everyday context and environment for the residents, helping to provide a continuation of their everyday lifestyle.

Two of the households are discreetly serviced via the service block but the other two require access from this service block to be via another household or externally, which is preferred.

Normally **access to one household via another would not be allowed** but the climate of Western Australia allows outdoor spaces to be used, in this case for taking deliveries from a central storage area to an 'unconnected' household.

There is an open door policy between households so residents are free to visit the others. Different colour schemes (see introduction) and the different motifs in the joinery and fretwork give each household its own identity and help residents to recognise and identify where they are in the whole development.

Bedroom doors have different patterns to their panels, providing a subtle, tactile orientation device. **However this may be too subtle for some people.**

Two different floor layouts also help with orientation adding interest and variety. The intention is that residents would be able to recognise if the household layout is their own, or not. Independent front doors to each household are very popular, families are given their own key and can come and go as they wish, as they could if visiting relatives in their own home. The formal lounge is used as a quiet room, family room and informal meeting space and has the appearance of a traditional front room, traditionally not used on a daily basis but only used for visitors. Birralee continues this tradition.

The 'Y'-shaped layouts are larger in area due to a larger open plan kitchen/dining/lounge than the linear households. The kitchen is located as the focal point, and has views over all communal lounge, dining, corridor and garden areas. With the kitchen visible from all the communal areas this helps residents to orientate themselves as they can always see the kitchen. Staff can also discreetly monitor residents.

Spaces, internally and externally, are domestic and intimate in scale and appearance is of familiar materials and shapes.

Bedrooms have either a corner window facing the rear garden areas or a small additional window with a direct view out to the front.

Most houses do not have a nurse station but have a study. The staff base is therefore referred to as the 'study' and domestic-looking windows allow staff to monitor residents discreetly.

There are no dead ends in Birralee; all corridors end in an alcove with access to the communal garden areas around the back of the building. The gardens themselves are well-established and well-maintained providing open, shaded, sitting or active opportunities for all the residents. As access is free around the building, residents can move according to the sun and the time of day.

Birralee creates a small village community atmosphere with the village square acting as the focus for the community. For people with dementia who have grown up in small communities this is a continuation of a lifestyle and environment with which they are familiar. No dead-ends and the layouts, colours and motifs of each household create an identity for each and therefore help residents to identify where they are in the overall development.

Bedroom corridor: Different colour scheme (see introduction) and motifs identify this household from others. The cupboard door is painted out to become 'invisible'. Different patterns of panels on bedroom doors aid orientation and identification. It is debatable if this is too subtle a cue for some people.

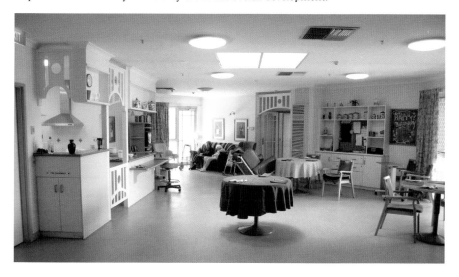

Kitchen/Dining to 'Y' shaped household: Kitchen location acts as a focus allowing residents to orientate themselves within the household because they can always see the kitchen. **This space looks empty because of the continuous floor and ceiling surfaces with nothing to break up the space.**

Bolltorpsgarden

BOLLTORPSGARDEN HOME
Bolltorpsvagen/Ginstgatan
Alingsas
Sweden

Contact for further information
Maude Ostlund, Glantz Architects, maude@glantzark.se

Owner AB Alingsashem

Website www.glantzark.se

View from street

Open since
September 2004

Architect
Glantz Arkitektstudio AB

Resident profile
24 residents with dementia and 4 respite care residents.
There is a children's day centre on part of the site for 80 children.

Number of residents
Three households of eight residents.
Four respite care rooms are connected to the day-care centre.
28 residents total.

Typical bedroom floor area
25.5sq.m plus 5.5sq.m en-suite: 31sq.m total

Floor area of each household
396sq.m

Building density
62.2sq.m per resident

Site area
3360sq.m (excluding school areas)

Courtyard garden: raised planters and greenhouse for residents' use.

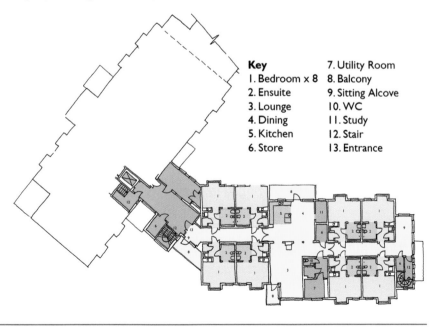

Key

1. Bedroom x 8
2. Ensuite
3. Lounge
4. Dining
5. Kitchen
6. Store
7. Utility Room
8. Balcony
9. Sitting Alcove
10. WC
11. Study
12. Stair
13. Entrance

Site density
120sq.m per resident

Staffing
Information not available.

Service and ancillary space
Each household has a kitchen and a staff access only utility room, wc and sluice. The staff base is located as a room off the dining area. Service rooms are located on the ground floor of the west side of the building, along with the respite care and day-care areas. The staff room is also located here and is large enough for training or large meetings.

There is a scooter storage area accessed externally near the front door.

Meals and laundry
Meals have the basic cooking/preparation done elsewhere and are then brought to each household. Within each kitchen the meals are completed by staff, with residents helping in final meal preparation, as far as they are able to. A central island in the kitchen/dining area with a low worktop allows residents to sit and be involved with kitchen activities. Most of the food is prepared in the main kitchen.

All laundry is done within each household by the staff. Residents can fold towels and clothing only.

Site context
Suburban sloping site in a small town in central Sweden.

Philosophy of care
AB Alingsashem, as an organisation, *works with municipal authorities in actively developing the provision of social services within small scale communities. Quality, working environment, natural environment and economy within program are all issues which are addressed.*

Lounge: 'Calm' green colour walls on one plane, neutral on perpendicular planes allows corners to be clearly defined. Upholstery contrasts with floor and wall/floor junctions which are also clearly-defined. There is no pattern to the upholstery and this makes a good contrast with the floor. **Polished timber floor could be perceived as wet but polished timber floors are common in Sweden and as such reflections like this are familiar to people here.**

Bedroom: Two doors to en-suite; en-suite hallway door is hinged, en-suite bedroom door is a sliding door. **This could present a problem if a resident tries to push or pull a sliding door.** Small kitchenette for making drinks or snacks, Services to here can be disconnected if required.

Bedroom corridor: Door contrasts with architraves and surrounding colour wall panel. Letter rack and switches contrast with this wall panel helping them to be seen. Coloured wall at end helps with orientation as a clear 'target'. Floor and wall junctions are clearly-defined. **Ceiling tiles, vinyl flooring and bedroom doors that are flush with corridor walls detract from the otherwise domestic appearance throughout the building. Having to fix residents' names to the doors highlights difficulties with residents identifying their own rooms.**

The aim is to contribute to the development of a lasting community. This is achieved by:
- *Getting to know present and future residents through personal meetings*
- *Quality of all operations is achieved through correct knowledge, experience and suitability*
- *Achieving value for money through economics of resources*
- *Working constantly on improvements and taking a positive view of development in order to meet future needs*
- *Creating a workplace with respect for each other and collaboration between staff*
- *Following current legal provisions.*

Philosophy expression in the building design
The building achieves a domestic scale environment where residents feel secure and can enjoy themselves. The design creates a feeling of wellbeing for the residents with comfortable spaces.

This building provides for a noisy, more exposed environment on the school side and a more private garden for elderly people. Residents have the choice of living on the 'quiet' or 'noisy' side of the building. Much use was made of research carried out on colour and visual perception and dementia, (see below).

Aspects of the building design that work well and which are worth repeating
The use of colour (see introduction) and colour contrast to the internal finishes. Greenhouse to the garden area allows use of external spaces during severe or inclement weather.

Kitchen/Dining: 'Active' colour and a neutral colour on walls. The central kitchen island allows residents to be involved with kitchen activities. Staff base is in room through the red wall.

Other comments
Upper floors have access to the garden via the central entrance hall, which is closed off to residents, therefore residents to two of the three households wishing to use the garden have to be accompanied by a member of staff.

AUTHOR'S COMMENT
The outstanding feature of this home is the careful and thorough consideration and use of colour and colour contrasts. This was based on research carried out by Helle Wijk (2001) at Gothenburg University on colour perception, old age and dementia, and subsequent dialogue with the architects for this project. Colour contrast is the primary consideration, colour itself is secondary to contrast.

There is vinyl flooring and timber flooring but no great contrast between the two, so there is no perception of a change in floor colour being perceived as a step. There are no metal edging strips between the floor finishes.

Ensuite: Sanitary ware, grabrails, cupboard door handles and shower all contrast with tiled wall and cupboard doors.

Wall colours are neutral on one plane, colour on the perpendicular plane. Therefore corners can be easily perceived by someone with impaired vision. Green, as a calming colour, is used in the lounge and sitting areas, red as a more active colour in kitchen/dining areas. The view down corridors is of a coloured wall, either red or green, which aids orientation.

Wall/floor junctions are clearly defined. Upholstery stands out from the floor so seats and table tops are obvious. There are no patterns in upholstery or other finishes, which can cause confusion.

Sockets, light switches, handrails, etc stand out from the wall behind. The window cill detail throughout is of thick limestone – a slot allows heat from the radiator to escape and the cill is wide enough for placing potted plants and sturdy enough to act as a grab rail. The cill is low enough to allow unobstructed views to the outside world when sitting.

Doors not accessible to residents are painted to blend in with surrounding walls. The doors into each household are glazed with obscured glass.

Bedroom doors are coloured, surrounding architrave contrasts and these doors have a further coloured surround. Within this surround are light switches, call buttons, letter rack, etc, which contrast and stand out from the background.

The bedrooms are more akin to studio apartments than bedrooms, with each unit having an entrance hall, storage, shower room and lounge/bedroom.

Each resident's room is large enough to be divided into a sleeping area and living area. Each room has a walk-in bay window in the living area and a second window allowing views from the bed. The kitchenette allows drinks and snacks to be made, either by the residents or family and visitors, and the water and electricity can be disconnected independently if required. Providing this ensures that residents can still maintain a degree of independence, not having to go down to the kitchen for a drink or snack.

The generously sized hallway has a hat and coat stand and walk-in storage and the door has an openable half-leaf for moving large items of furniture.

Each en-suite has two doors. There is no communal wc near the common areas so residents have to use their own en-suites. A hinged door is accessed from each 'apartment' hallway for ease of access when approaching from outside the unit, and there is also a sliding door from the sleeping area within each unit. This door slides into the wall structure, creating free wall space. Sliding doors are common in Scandinavia and more familiar to people there than elsewhere. Within the en-suite, there is coloured tiling to contrast with the sanitary ware, toilet roll holder is black to contrast, and cupboard door knobs contrast with the cupboard door.

The main lounge and dining/kitchen are placed centrally to the household to break up the run of corridor and each half of the corridor is also staggered to avoid a clear line of sight right through. The corridors end in either an informal sitting alcove or a small sitting area with a balcony. Therefore there are no dead ends but 'events' at the corridor ends.

There are plain ceilings in bedrooms and informal sitting areas but suspended ceilings in corridor, main lounge and kitchen/dining areas. Patterns in the ceiling and use of drop lighting help reduce any institutional impact of this.

There are also three balconies on the upper floors, from one end of the bedroom corridor, from the lounge area and from the dining area. Therefore there are different views, either outwards to the street or children's centre, or inwards to the garden area. Ground floor residents have direct access to the garden area from their dining area.

The garden is enclosed by buildings on two sides with a retaining wall and a grass embankment and fencing on the fourth side. There are raised planting beds on the retaining wall, which in time will be covered in ivy and other climbing plants. The raised beds allow residents to sit and work with planting and gardening activities. A path around the garden is a figure-of-eight pattern and raised edging allows for seating, as well as the seating areas being provided. This also accommodates the change in level across the garden. A greenhouse has been provided and will allow residents to undertake gardening activities during the winter.

This home has had a lot of careful thought applied to the design and finishes. The corridor areas could have had the residents doors recessed to create the impression of a front porch.

One of the reasons for Bolltorpsgarden's success lies in the carefully thought-out use of colour contrast; there is much to be learnt from this which could be applied elsewhere.

➤ **It is disappointing however that staff and residents have had to stick their own improvised name signs on to these doors.**

➤ **There is the possibility of someone with impaired reasoning not recognising a sliding door and trying to push or pull it.**

➤ **As it stands, the corridor areas do have something of a hospital appearance.**

Charnwood House

CHARNWOOD HOUSE
77a Beake Avenue
Radford
Coventry
CV6 3AQ
Great Britain

Contact for further information
Dawn Hancox, Home Manager home.cov@mha.org.uk

Owner Methodist Homes for the Aged (MHA)

Website www.mha.org.uk

Variety in planting provides stimulation in colours and texture. Railing in fence allow views in and out of adjoining park from garden areas and lounge areas. Walking path loops around building but always leads back inside, avoiding any dead ends. Different gazebos located throughout all the garden areas help with orientation and walking pathways provide choice. Overall appearance is of a domestic scale.

Open since
February 2004

Architect
Carless and Adams Partnership, Slough

Resident profile
45 residents with dementia (all levels of dementia)
12 residents with early stages of dementia (respite/intermediate care)

Number of residents
Three households of 15 residents
One household of 12 residents (intermediate care)
57 residents total

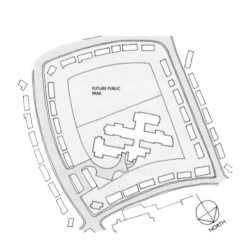

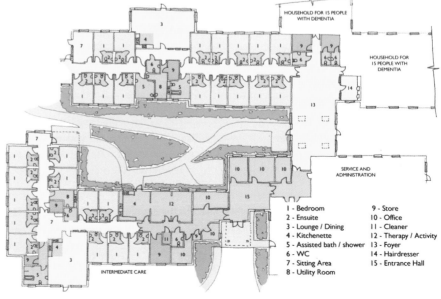

1 - Bedroom
2 - Ensuite
3 - Lounge / Dining
4 - Kitchenette
5 - Assisted bath / shower
6 - WC
7 - Sitting Area
8 - Utility Room
9 - Store
10 - Office
11 - Cleaner
12 - Therapy / Activity
13 - Foyer
14 - Hairdresser
15 - Entrance Hall

Typical bedroom floor area
14.5sq.m plus 2.8sq.m en-suite: 17.3sq.m

Floor area for each household
525sq.m for 15 resident household
415sq.m for 12 resident household

Building density
46sq.m /resident

Site area
10,800sq.m

Site density
189sq.m/resdient

Staffing
The staff ratio is one care staff to every five residents.
The care staff provide care and helping with everyday living tasks. Additionally there are domestic, and laundry staff, a cook and kitchen assistants, a maintenance worker, an administration assistant, assistant manager and manager. There is also an activities co-coordinator.

Service and ancillary space
Each household has a kitchenette in the lounge/dining area. There is a central kitchen and laundry, staff facilities and administration.

Meals and laundry
All meals are served in the dining/lounge area in each household. Breakfast, high tea, supper and snacks are prepared in each kitchenette area with the main meal of the day prepared in the central kitchen and brought to each household. Residents are consulted regarding menus.

Communal lounge: Chairs in the middle of the room are not popular as people like to sit with their back to a wall or other fixed object. Curtains, fireplace surround with mirror over and light fittings are of a style familiar to this generation of people.

Dining and kitchenette area in household:
Domestic kitchen cupboards and fittings (apart from the paper towel dispenser) are all familiar. Analogue wall clock is also more familiar than a digital clock. Chairs on runners allow them to be moved (slide) across carpet more easily and are also less likely to tip over if someone leans on the armrest.

The intermediate care household has a separate full kitchen for use by the residents. By preparing meals with staff, the staff can assess their daily living skills in a subtle, unobtrusive manner.

All clothing and linen is cleaned in the central laundry. Residents help with folding, sorting and storing items of clothing.

Site context
Backland site in an inner suburb of Coventry.

Philosophy of care
MHA mission and values statement is:

We are a charity striving to combine professional standards, top class management and financial sustainability in providing older people with a caring service based on Christian principles. Our values underpin all our work which may be summarised as:

- *High quality, person-centred care and support for older people*
- *Founded on compassion and respect for individuals' dignity and personal choice*
- *Focused on nurturing a person's spiritual and physical well-being.*

Philosophy expression in the building design
Charnwood House aims to create a calm, relaxed and reassuring atmosphere. The building design allows this to happen by:

- *The size and scale of the building and the spaces are all of a domestic quality. Fixtures and fittings such as lights and taps are also familiar and recognizable. There are no dead-ends, all communal spaces have doors to the secure outside garden areas and all paths lead back inside the building.*

- *The open door policy between the three households allows residents to visit friends in the other households, as if one were visiting a friend in the next street. This is between the three households of people with dementia; the intermediate care unit is a separate entity.*

• With a kitchenette open to the dining/living area residents can freely use the kitchenette for making snacks or drinks; the sounds and smells of meal preparation are activities and stimuli that occur in all domestic households.

• The open foyer allows for a more informal space than a separate function or multi-purpose room. A resident can more easily slip in or out of something happening here without self-consciously opening/closing doors and potentially causing a distraction.

Aspects of the building design that work well and which are worth repeating
• The open door access between households.
• The open door access to the outside garden spaces
• The freedom to potter about doing everyday things and making a contribution to the daily life of the household. The building layout and design allows this to happen
• Glazed panels in doors to lounges, sitting areas, etc
• Deliveries kept away from residents areas to avoid distraction and disruption

Other comments
Separating the intermediate care from the other three households is not ideal, however as the intermediate care is for people with early stages of dementia, it is debatable if full integration would work.

Fire regulations require fire doors between households and the foyer, along the bedroom corridors and to separate the lounge/dining areas from the corridors. Ideally these would be removed and have an open access

There are two sitting areas at the end of the bedroom corridors. The window alcove is popular but the separate sitting room area is not used much by residents. Instead they are used for private meetings with families or informal staff meetings.

AUTHOR'S COMMENTS
Charnwood House has a relaxed and welcoming feel, the spaces are of a comfortable domestic scale and the building, staff, activities and care are all aimed at achieving as a 'normal' lifestyle as possible for the residents.

For the intermediate care household, it is very important to these residents that their immediate environment is familiar as they may not have the time to readjust and relearn to new and unfamiliar things.

The foyer area between three of the households serves as the multi-purpose area where large

Bedroom corridor: Different colour doors help residents with identifying which door is theirs but the use of objects or memory boxes would be better as colour perception can diminish with old age. The details of the skirting boards, architraves and mouldings with carpeting and a plain ceiling finish give a domestic feel. Ceiling lighting is emergency lighting only, wall-lights provide an even, glare free lighting and are high enough on the wall so as not to be a hazard to residents.

En-suite: Sanitary ware contrast well with walls **although white grab rail against white tiling may be difficult to see.** Toilet can be seen from bed. Traditional crosshead taps are more familiar than modern lever taps.

However, the location of this space does ◄ mean that an activity or event occurring here will dominate any other interaction between the three households. Access to the three households from the administration and service block is also through this space and an activity taking place here could be disrupted or distracted by comings and goings from the administration and service block.

activities and events can take place. The advantage of this is doing away with a separate room and, as stated above, residents can enter or leave the activity or event with less likelihood of being noticed by other residents if doors are opening and closing. There is also a hairdresser's salon located off the foyer space.

The open door policy allows residents to feel they are part of a larger community; each resident has the opportunity to talk to or interact with another 30 people at any time they want outside their immediate circle of 15. Different colour schemes (see introduction) in each household and different names and nameplates help identify each household and aid orientation. There is the opportunity to build on the household names with objects to give identity, e.g. the 'willow' household could use willow leaves as a motif, the 'sycamore' household likewise. This could also extend externally into the garden areas.

Each bedroom door is a different colour (see introduction) to help orientation and a nameplate and photograph provide visual cues. Doors, handrails and walls all have good colour contrast. Handrails have a small raised button as a tactile warning that the handrail is about to end or turn a corner. All toilet doors are a shade of pink **but the tone is probably too subtle to be recognizable by someone with poor eyesight.**

Carpets are used throughout which is a familiar floor finish for the UK. The carpet is continuous with no sharp contrasts which could create the illusion of a step.

Plain painted plasterboard ceilings are also used throughout, which is a conventional domestic feature. In a single storey building services can be accessed through the roof space so a suspended ceiling is not necessary.

The lounge/dining/kitchenette area is well used with curtains, fireplace and kitchen cupboards of a familiar appearance to the resident group here. There is a continuous line of windows and a door to the outside, glazed panels to the corridor allowing sight of activity passing by as well as a view to the toilet accessed from the corridor. Each lounge has a different view outside, which also helps residents with orientation and distinguishes between each household.

There are a lot of ornamental ceiling lights in the lounge/dining area, providing much brightness but creating a somewhat cluttered ceiling. Wall lights in the corridor areas provide subdued, even lighting as well as breaking up areas of blank wall.

The kitchen units in the kitchenette area are all domestic in appearance **but have solid doors.** Transparent doors would allow a view of the contents and avoid confusion if a resident cannot remember which items are stored where.

A change in direction in the bedroom corridors avoids the impression of an endlessly long corridor. In the intermediate care household at this change in direction the corridor itself is widened to create an informal seating area. However this is little used because of the lack of natural light. The seating alcove at the end of the bedroom corridors with a fixed bench seat is popular but the separate sitting room located here is little used, probably because it is away from any activity. However it does serve a purpose for private meetings.

Bedrooms are well-proportioned with views over garden areas. Window cills are a standard height and would benefit by being lower to allow more views outside from the bed. The wc can be seen from the bed and the walls are not fully tiled allowing for the non-tiled wall areas to be colour painted, helping to create a more domestic appearance. A small lockable cupboard allows residents to store valuables.

Whilst there is a medicine store and general office, there is no fixed staff base within each household. There is a trolley that is brought out and stored away as required and this contains files and records. Staff can move this trolley about depending on what may be happening at any one time. If all the residents are in the garden, for example, the staff can be outside too whilst writing up notes.

The service and administration block contains the central kitchen, laundry, staff and office facilities. There are no views of deliveries or the main entrance from the three dementia households but the residents receiving intermediate care do have a view of the entrance area and car park. The entrance hall and front door is between the administration block and the intermediate care household.

Externally, each garden area is slightly different with seating gazebos and differing planting beds offering cues to orientation. All paths lead back into each household, either at the end of the bedroom corridor or the lounge. There are no raised planting beds at present but there are plans to construct some in the near future.

External paved areas are in black tarmac for the pathways but seating areas are buff coloured paving flags.

To the west boundary a public park will be built. On this boundary there is close boarded fencing but gaps in the fencing with railings will allow residents to see into the park from the lounge areas as well as letting the public see into the development.

Charnwood House has set out to create an environment that allows residents to continue with their normal everyday life. Overall this has been achieved and the relaxed and happy atmosphere to the households speaks for itself.

Handrail contrasts well with walls and returning the handrail to the wall avoids the risk of snagging clothing on a blunt end. Raised buttons provide a tactile cue that there is a change in direction or end of the handrail. **The bright finish to the raised button results in some residents trying to pick them off.**

➤ **There are no distinct edges to the hard and soft areas but there are also no reports of residents walking off the hard surfaces or finding difficulty with the change in paving material.**

Charnwood Lodge

REASONS FOR SELECTION

➤ Entrance area used as multi-purpose space
➤ Calm and relaxed atmosphere in a busy location
➤ Finishes, fixtures and fittings create a homely atmosphere
➤ Sensory garden

CHARNWOOD LODGE
8-18 Annan Road
Dumfries
DG1 3AD
Scotland
Great Britain

Contact for further information
Shirley McTier, Home Manager
charnwoodlodge@c-i-c.co.uk

Owner Community Integrated Care (CIC)

Website www.c-i-c.co.uk

Garden area: South facing to maximise daylight and plenty of open space, paths, seating areas and familiar objects such as the streetlight. Raised planting beds are for ease of working at when sitting. Bench seating with arms is essential for residents to sit at comfortably.

Open since
1998

Architect
Robert Potter and Partners, Dumfries

Resident profile
37 residents who are frail and elderly and require palliative care
20 residents who have dementia or challenging behaviour
3 residents who require respite care
There is an adjoining day centre.

Number of residents
6 households of 10 residents
60 residents total

Typical bedroom floor area
13.4sq.m plus 4.1sq.m en-suite: 17.5sq.m

Floor area for each household
321sq.m

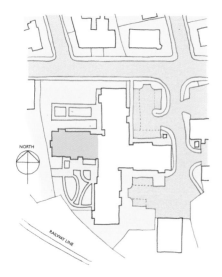

1 - Bedroom x 10	6 - Sitting Area	11 - Store
2 - Ensuite	7 - WC	12 - Emergency Exit
3 - Dining	8 - Shower	13 - Sluice
4 - Kitchenette	9 - Assisted Bath	14 - Communal Hall
5 - Lounge	10 - Window Seat	

The cinema area located off of the main entrance foyer. An opening in the wall without a door allows residents to enter and leave without the distraction of opening and closing doors. The entrance foyer beyond is also used as a multi-purpose space. This entrance foyer space is big enough for larger events to take place whilst still allowing circulation of daily activities. A sitting area located by window allows views of entrance, car park and outside activity, as well as the activity within.

Lounge in each household: Familiar finishes and objects such as carpets, curtains, furniture, light fittings, fireplace along with non-patterned surfaces and a plain ceiling create the feel of a domestic front room.

Building density
58sq.m /resident

Site area
3870sq.m

Site density
64.5sq.m / resident

Staffing
There are 17 care staff, one service manager and one assistant service manager plus domestic staff, cleaners, kitchen staff and maintenance

Service and ancillary space
In each household there is a kitchenette, bathroom, showeroom and sluice. There is a central kitchen and laundry.

Meals and laundry
Lunch and dinner are prepared in the main kitchen and brought to each household where it is served in the dining room. Breakfast, supper, drinks and snacks are prepared in the kitchenette in each household.

All laundry is done in the main laundry on the ground floor.

Site context
Flat site close to the town centre of Dumfries, sandwiched between a busy road and a railway line

Philosophy of care
Community Integrated Care's mission statement is *"Putting Individuals First"* and their vision is:
- *To deliver agreed person-centred services which add value to the lives of the people we support, involving their family, friends, advocates and the local community where possible*
- *To be a market leader in providing high quality and innovative support packages for individuals who have a learning disability, mental health need or require high dependency nursing or social care.*

Kitchenette off dining room: Change in floor colours are of a similar tone. **Cupboard doors do not make it obvious what is inside. Sink tap and paper towel dispenser are not domestic in appearance.**

Window seat alcove at end of corridor creates an 'event' and not a dead end. Someone sitting here would be facing back down the way they came which helps with orientation. **If the ceiling were lowered over the alcove area and were not a lay-in grid suspended ceiling then a more intimate space could be created.** The carpet is different colours between households (see introduction) helping to identify each household

- *For all trustees and employees to be committed to the success of the organization and to feel a valued member of the team.*
- *To provide the highest level of appropriate training, education and the development of the staff team.*
- *To ensure, through effective management, that the maximum value of the charity's resources are directed towards enhancing the quality of life of our service users.*

Philosophy expression in the building design
- *Small domestic households of ten residents allow residents to feel more secure and to exercise a greater sense of control over their lives.*
- *Wide and well proportioned corridors (two metres) give a sense of space and openness.*
- *Size of bedrooms allows residents own furniture, ornaments and personal possessions to be brought in, helping to reinforce the home-from-home atmosphere.*

Aspects of the building design that work well and which are worth repeating
- *Access to the garden areas from the ground floor households is very popular*
- *Window seat at the end of corridors with views outside. Varity in these window seats helps with orientation*
- *The generous width of corridors promotes a feeling of space*
- *The cinema area off the entrance foyer is very well used*
- *The sensory garden is also popular*

Other comments
En-suite rooms have a toilet and washbasin only, no shower. There is one shower and one bath shared between ten people, which is unusual. Most facilities include a shower in the en-suite and have a single bath shared amongst each household. The staff at Charnwood Lodge have decorated some of the communal areas themselves, with consultation and help from residents and their families and this does help to give a personal identity to each household.

AUTHOR'S COMMENTS
Charnwood Lodge is a modest scheme, the building itself acts as the backdrop allowing for a relaxed atmosphere. Whilst there are no outstanding features the overall impression is of homely domesticity.

The entrance foyer acts as a multi-purpose space with large group events taking place in this area. This space is large enough to accommodate many people without allowing other comings and goings to distract. By not having events in a room behind a door, residents can more easily come and go without the distraction of doors opening and closing. However, when not being used for a large event this space does feel empty, with clusters of furniture in the corners and a large empty space in the middle. Residents appear to prefer to stay within the smaller scale spaces of each household.

To one side of the entrance foyer a cinema area has been created. There is a screen to separate it from the rest of the foyer but no door, allowing people to come and go more easily. This is very popular as a quiet area or meeting room when films are not being shown.

The corridor spaces within each household at two metres wide are sufficient to give an impres-

Sitting area adjacent to the lounge: This is more popular than the lounge probably because daily activity can be observed more easily. Ground floor has access to garden, first floor has overlooking windows. Bedroom doors have numbers, name plate and picture frame to act as multiple cues to help residents identify their own room. **Sharp contrast in carpet could be perceived as a step by some people with dementia.**

sion of space and are well proportioned so as not to feel too wide and uncomfortable. At the end there is a seating bench built into a bay window and the seat looks back down the corridor and windows on either side allow views out. Each bay window and window seat is slightly different which helps residents to identify which household they are in. Generally the doors to each household from the entrance foyer are left open unless there are would be a risk to a resident in doing this.

➤ These doors are not very domestic in their appearance.

There is a 'formal' lounge in each household which is little used; most residents prefer to spend time in the open sitting area adjacent to the lounge, probably because activity within the household can be seen more easily. On the ground floor there is also access to the garden from here. There are views over the garden areas from the first floor sitting area in each household.

The dining area is a separate room and the kitchenette is also located here. The ground floor households also have access to the garden spaces from here. The kitchen cupboards are all typically domestic in style. With the kitchen open to the dining area this allows for kitchen activities and associated noise and smell to stimulate any residents in the dining area. Timber and glass screens to the lounge and dining areas allow daylight to penetrate the corridors further adding to the sense of space and also allowing views into any activity taking place.

➤ However, as the kitchen/dining is a separate room, any kitchen activity and stimulation is confined to the dining area.

All these spaces are well proportioned, make good use of natural daylight and the use of carpets and domestic, familiar decorations, furniture, fixtures and fittings go a long way to creating the homely atmosphere. Lounge, dining and bedroom areas do have a more domestic plain ceiling.

➤ The lay-in grid suspended ceiling in the corridor areas is not a familiar domestic finish; however, one could argue that people don't generally spend their time looking up at the ceiling when walking along a corridor.

The vinyl flooring to the kitchenette and the carpet in the dining room are of a similar tone which overcomes any potential perception of a 'step' created by a sharp contrast. The carpets continue into the bedrooms from the corridors, also avoiding the perception of a step or barrier. A brass edging strip on the floor at the bedroom door does not appear to be perceived as a barrier.

Traditional-looking wall-lights help to break up the appearance of long blank walls and provide a variety in lighting options. For example, at night just the wall lights are turned on, for a more subdued effect.

The bedrooms are larger than the minimum requirements of the Regulation of Care (Scotland) Act 2001. The doors have photo frames fixed to the door along with a name plate and door number, providing multiple cues for residents to identify their own door. Some residents have chosen to have the photo frame removed from their door.

The position of the toilet means that it can be seen from the bed, which is important for some people with impaired memory who may forget to use the toilet unless they can see it. The current Scottish National Care Standards require new care homes to have en-suite bath or shower facilities.

➤ The absence of a shower in the en-suite is questionable. Residents having to leave their room and walk down a corridor past other residents in order to have a shower, has institutional overtones. It should also be noted that at the time of construction, regulations required en-suites to have a toilet and washbasin as a minimum; a shower was not a requirement.

A sensory garden has been built on the ground floor with direct access from the two ground floor households and the entrance foyer. There is a generous seating area and a looped path. This path is of a bonded gravel which is not reported to be a problem with frail residents walking on this type of surface. Raised planting beds, seating areas, garden ornaments such as a bird table and a traditional-looking ornamental streetlight and a variety of planting provide a full sensory experience. The residents and staff were involved in the design and construction of the sensory garden and the ongoing maintenance is one of the activities undertaken by residents.

The rear boundary wall is made from local stone and dates from when the adjoining railway was built. This in itself is a familiar appearance and texture to many of the residents as most of the town has been constructed from this type of stone. Mature trees on the rear boundary have been pruned recently allowing more daylight into the garden area.

Staff have reported that the noise and regular frequency of passing trains is in itself a source of interest and stimulation with the residents. The punctuality, or not, of the Carlisle to Glasgow service is often a topic of discussion! It is interesting that what may have been thought of as a potential noise problem has turned out to be a means of contact with the world.

Charnwood Lodge does not set out to make a grand statement, either architecturally or in terms of dementia design. This scheme has created comfortable spaces with a human and familiar scale and proportion, and achieved this on a site bounded by a busy road and a railway line. The building design along with the care delivered by the staff creates the homely, relaxed atmosphere.

Daelhoven & De Wiekslag

Reasons for selection
- ➤ **Family sized households of six residents**
- ➤ **Staff have multi-task roles**
- ➤ **Village square concept to Daelhoven**
- ➤ **Integration of both homes with the local community**

DAELHOVEN
Graanakker 11
3762 BS
Soest
Netherlands

Contact for further information
Ad Witlock, Director secretariaat@daelhoven.nl

Owner Zorgpalet Baarn-Soest

Website www.zorgpaletbaarnsoest.nl/daelhoven.htm

Daelhoven Village Square: The staircase is hidden behind the clock tower, which is in the style of a railway station. Canopy contains a smoke extractor hood and this is the designated smoking area. Daylight, brick paviours, external style street lights, outdoor café furniture gives an outdoor quality to this space. The roof can open out in good weather.

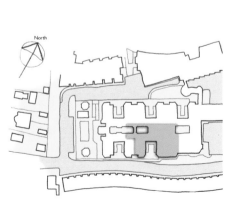

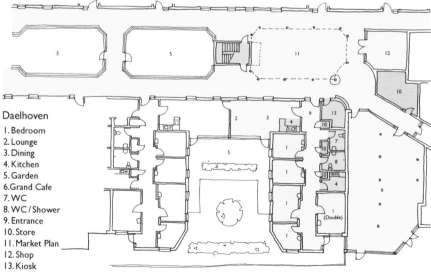

Daelhoven
1. Bedroom
2. Lounge
3. Dining
4. Kitchen
5. Garden
6. Grand Cafe
7. WC
8. WC / Shower
9. Entrance
10. Store
11. Market Plan
12. Shop
13. Kiosk

DE WIEKSLAG
Veenbesstraat 1
Soest
Netherlands

Contact for further information
Ad Witlock, Director secretariaat@daelhoven.nl

Owner Zorgpalet Baarn-Soest

Website www.zorgpaletbaarnsoest.nl/de_wiekslag.htm

De Wiekslag: Care home on left, primary school on right. Care home is on the ground floor, sheltered housing apartments are located on the first floor.

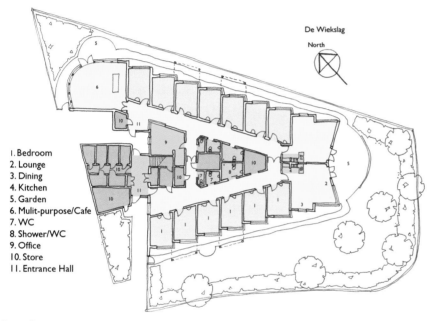

De Wiekslag

North

1. Bedroom
2. Lounge
3. Dining
4. Kitchen
5. Garden
6. Mulit-purpose/Cafe
7. WC
8. Shower/WC
9. Office
10. Store
11. Entrance Hall

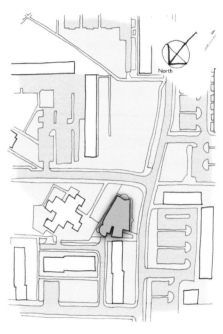

North

Open since
Daelhoven: 1997
De Wiekslag: 1999

Architect
Henk Overeem, Robert Kromhof
Jorissen Simonetti Architecten

Resident profile
Daelhoven: Ten households of six residents with dementia.
Three households of six residents with physical disabilities.
Two households of six residents requiring rehabilitation treatment.
De Wiekslag: 2 households of 6 residents with dementia.

Number of residents
Daelhoven: 60 residents with dementia.
18 residents with physical disabilities.
12 residents requiring rehabilitation treatment.
90 residents total.
De Wiekslag: 12 residents with dementia.

Typical bedroom floor area
Daelhoven: 13.5sq.m (no en-suite)
De Wiekslag: 16.9sq.m (no en-suite)

Floor area of each household
Daelhoven: 225
De Wiekslag: 235sq.m

Daelhoven: Front door of household. Display cabinet, household number, nameplate, clear colours (see introduction) and hanging object offer multiple cues for residents to identify this as their household. Brick walls, wall light and style of front door reinforce the impression of a front door with a private household within. Visitors have to knock and wait to be let in as in any other private house.

Building density
Daelhoven: 61sq.m /resident
De Wiekslag: 58sq.m /resident

Site area
Daelhoven: 6980sq.m
De Wiekslag: 1665sq.m

Site density
Daelhoven: 77.5sq.m /resident
De Wiekslag: 139sq.m /resident

Staffing

Daelhoven:	Six management staff
	10.5 full-time care staff between 12 residents (ie two households): 78 total
	90 full-time and part-time ancillary staff
De Wiekslag:	Ten full-time care staff total
	1.5 additional medical and support staff

Each household of six residents has two members of staff during the day and students from local schools provide additional support from 4:30pm-7:30pm and at other busy times. This is also part of integrating into the community, educating youngsters about people with dementia or physical disabilities and bringing the local community into the lives of the people who live here.

Service and ancillary space

| Daelhoven: | Each household has its own kitchen, wc and shower-room. There is a staff room shared between two households. |
| | There is also a café, supermarket, kiosk, chapel, multi-sensory room, internet café, hairdresser and separate activities room all located next to the central village square. |

Daelhoven: Kiosk and notice pillar in the Village Square – further creating the impression of an outdoor space. The lower ceiling creates a more intimate space by household flat doors and the kiosk. There is also a shop where residents from each household can use, or use the shops and market in the town.

Located at the front of the building are the main reception area, staff restaurant, changing facilities, workshop and the main administration offices for the care homes in the Soest area.

De Wiekslag: Each household has its own kitchen and a central core contains 2 wc and shower rooms for each household.

There is also a café with an outdoor terrace next to the adjoining school playground and a staff office. Secure bicycle stores are also provided, and a tandem bicycle is available for residents and staff to visit the local shops and market.

Meals and laundry

All meals are prepared and eaten within each household. Residents agree their own meals with staff and use the shop on site (Daelhoven) as well as helping with the preparation as far as they are able to. The multi-tasking staff, and often relatives, cook the meals. The smells and sounds of meal preparation provide stimulus for the residents and give structure to the day. At De Wiekslag, residents can accompany staff to the local shops and market to purchase food. Laundry and cleaning is undertaken within each household with residents helping the staff.

Site context

Daelhoven: Sloping site close to town centre
De Wiekslag: Flat site adjoining primary school and in the middle of a housing estate
Soest is a small town north-east of Utrecht.

Philosophy of care

Ad Witlock, Director writes:
"The underlying concept is to create a home-like and recognisable environment, both with-in the buildings and to the provision of care. Key words to this are:
* *Privacy and respect*
* *Recognisable and domestic*
* *Intimacy, security and familiarity*
* *Social contact*
* *Multi-disciplinary and integrated care*
* *Co-operative administration*

Integration with the community is also a key concept:
* *Students from the local school help out during the afternoon and during school holidays*
* *Residents are taken to and use the local swimming pool every Friday morning*
* *Residents and staff go shopping in the local market and shops*

De Wiekslag is next to a primary school, a recycling centre and a busy road junction: this location allows the activity of the neighbourhood to be observed.
160 volunteers are working for Daelhoven and De Wiekslag.

Daelhoven: Lounge/Dining in household. Proportion of the room is homely but the **ceiling detracts from an otherwise typically Dutch living room. Polished timber floor and reflections could also be problematic.**

De Wiekslag: Lounge/Dining and Kitchen area behind. Domestic scale of spaces and furniture create a homely atmosphere. Doors give access to garden area and large windows provide ample daylight. Each household does their own cooking in this kitchen.

Other activities include singing, walking, arts and crafts and an internet café.

Philosophy expression in the building design

Family sized households of six residents. Six is the size of a large family, any larger and the situation becomes group living. Each household is self-contained and independent with its own lounge, kitchen, bedrooms, toilets, showers, hallway and front door and is recognisable as a family house. Two households share a small garden area which looks out to the public streets and activity.

Daelhoven has a village square with familiar activities of a shop, café, and kiosk. The use of external materials and furniture, daylight and an openable roof create the feel of an outdoor space. The staircase is disguised as a railway station clock tower and there is even a railway timetable. The canopy here has an extractor fan so underneath has become the designated smoking area.

The café is a social focal point and is a familiar and common part of Dutch life.

The aim is to allow the residents to continue with their own way of life, as if they were still living in their own home. The family sized households, domestic environment and integration with the community allow this to happen.

Aspects of the building design that work well and which are worth repeating

The central village square in Daelhoven is the focus around which the whole facility revolves. Careful use of daylight, external materials and details makes these feel like external spaces.

The café in De Wiekslag and the outdoor terrace next to the school provide the focus for the residents. The location of De Wiekslag, in the middle of a housing estate, provides the opportunity for greater integration into the community and for residents to observe daily life going on around them.

The front door in each household looks like the front door to a house with doorbell, external light and memory box and a brick wall surround. These also offer multiple cues for residents to identify their own front door.

Other comments

There are no en-suite facilities to either home because few people would have them in their own home and have not lived previously with an en-suite bathroom. Therefore it would be an unfamiliar feature within these households. Sharing a bathroom with your family is a familiar situation and with households of six residents this is a family sized group. A larger group sharing bathrooms would present difficulties. There is a washbasin in each bedroom.

The first floor of De Wiekslag has sheltered housing apartments, accessed from a stairway from the entrance hall. For couples this allows one to be in the ground floor care home and the other, more able, partner to be nearby. Additionally, the advantages gained by the location of the building in relation to the town can also by enjoyed by the people living on the first floor.

De Wiekslag: Café/social hub of the building and is the social hub of the development. Hard floor surfaces and this style of furniture are typically Dutch. Other activities also take place here and this space is also used as a multi-function room.

AUTHOR'S COMMENT

Both Daelhoven and De Wiekslag are good examples of the Dutch approach to dementia care. Households of six residents are very small units compared to the more common household units ranging from ten to fourteen residents used in other countries, but six people is the size of a large family. By having each household self-contained in terms of its facilities and provision of care this is applying the concept of a 'familiar domestic environment' through all aspects of the home.

The Anton Pieck-Hofje in Haarlem, Netherlands (1990) was pioneering in allowing residents to continue their own lifestyles within a familiar, domestic environment. (see Judd *et al* 1998) Daelhoven and De Wiekslag have continued this idea, learnt from the experiences there and applied it to the current regulations.

The built environment of both these homes goes a long way to allow for a continuation of a resident's 'normal' lifestyle. The family-sized households, large windows providing views to the outside world from the lounge, garden and bedroom areas; familiar forms, materials and objects have all been designed in from the outset.

The location of these premises, bringing the community into the homes and taking residents out into the community is also a key factor in the success. Residents feel they are still part of, and can take part in, the daily life and routine of the community at large.

'Brown Cafes' are as much a community social hub in the Netherlands as the pub is in Britain. This space can be used as a multi-purpose room, allowing for activities such as concerts, singing, meetings, family visits in addition to its role as a café where a beer or coffee can be enjoyed in the company of others.

The Village Square in Daelhoven does have the look and feel of a small village square. Ample daylight, external paving flooring, brick walls and outdoor furniture set the scene. The roof can open up in summer to avoid excessive heat build-up and allow fresh air in. The shop displays its goods out into the square, as any other shop would. The kiosk, café, chapel and front doors to several of the households are all accessed from this space creating a true community feel. The staircase hidden behind the 'railway station' clock tower with a canopy and railway timetable is a nice touch. Integrating the smokers' extractor hood into the canopy resolves the issue of where to put smokers without making them feel isolated in a separate room. Again, this is typical of the philosophy of care creating a designed solution to a potential problem. Relating to the railway theme is a wall mounted display cabinet in the village square with displays of model railway trains and memorabilia.

Each house has its own door number in the style of a traditional door number plate along with a display cabinet, different colours and styles all offering multiple cues for those with impaired memory. A doorbell has to be rung to be allowed in, as in any other house. Apart from the front door there are no other cues or orientation devices within the household, the reason being that you would not have these in your own home and each household is of a small enough scale for people to become familiar with the layout.

On first impression the interiors of De Wiekslag seem bare, with suspended ceiling and vinyl flooring, but this is typical of many Dutch apartment blocks. Most of the residents are local and have lived a great part of their lives in the post-war apartment blocks. The ceilings to the living and bedroom areas are the painted underside of the concrete floor slab above, but again this is typical of Dutch houses and apartments. The interior finishes to Daelhoven are of suspended ceiling throughout and the households have a vinyl floor that looks like timber strip flooring. In the living rooms a genuine timber floor is used.

Both Daelhoven and De Wiekslag show how a philosophy of care can be applied to the design of the building and how that design facilitates and encourages the provision of care and the integration of the home within the community. The core concept of family sized households of six residents allows the daily life to operate as a family, rather than group living.

De Wiekslag: Typical bedroom. Bay window allows for two different views out. Residents' own furniture personalises each room. Full-height glazing also maximises daylight. **Glare on floor surface could be perceived as being wet.**

De Wiekslag: Patio terrace from café with views of school playground and neighbourhood activity. Residents spend much time here watching the school children and daily life of the neighbourhood, allowing them to feel part of the world and not isolated.

➤ **Reflections from a shiny floor can be perceived as being wet by some people with dementia but there have not been any reported problems here.**

Denville Hall

REASONS FOR SELECTION

➤ **Client-specific group**
➤ **Extension to existing building**
➤ **Innovative use of sloping site and external spaces**

DENVILLE HALL
62 Ducks Hill Road
Northwood
Middlesex
HA6 2SB
Great Britain

Contact for further information
Moira Miller, Manager moira.miller@btconnect.com

Owner The Actors Charitable Trust

Website www.denvillehall.org

Bedrooms facing lawn: There is a ramped access to lawn from the upper level that loops around the grounds as a pathway. (Photo by David Wrightson.)

Open since
New Build extension: May 2003
Refurbished existing building: March 2004

Architect
Acanthus LW, Chiswick, London

Resident profile
One household of 15 residents with dementia on the ground floor of the new building only. 25 residents requiring nursing or residential care are on the first floor of the existing and new building.

Number of residents
15 residents with dementia
25 residents requiring nursing or residential care
40 residents total

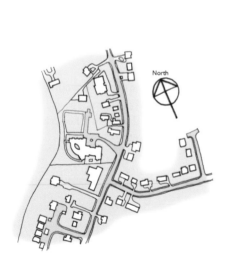

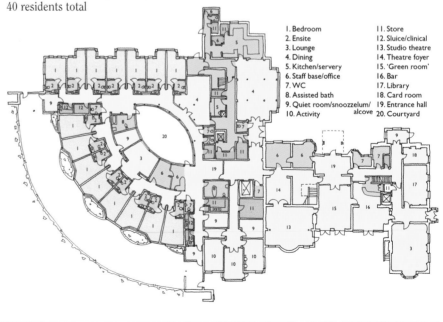

1. Bedroom
2. Ensite
3. Lounge
4. Dining
5. Kitchen/servery
6. Staff base/office
7. WC
8. Assisted bath
9. Quiet room/snoozzelum/
10. Activity

11. Store
12. Sluice/clinical
13. Studio theatre
14. Theatre foyer
15. 'Green room'
16. Bar
17. Library
18. Card room
19. Entrance hall
20. Courtyard
alcove

Typical bedroom floor area
16.6sq.m plus 4.4sq.m en-suite: 21sq.m total

Floor area of each household
766sq.m to the dementia specific household
(footprint area of the ground floor extension 1159sq.m)

Building density
79sq.m /resident (new extension and existing building)

Site area
12,400sq.m

Site density
310sq.m /resident

Staffing
There are three administration and management staff

The household for people with dementia, known as Jeanne's wing, has a staffing ratio of 4:1 during the day of one nurse and three care assistants. The nursing/residential household has one nurse and five to six care staff during the day.

Overnight there is one nurse for both households plus two care staff for the nursing/residential household and two-three staff for the dementia household, depending on need.

Additionally there are nine cleaning staff, two maintenance staff, a part-time gardener and the catering is sub-contracted

Service and ancillary space
On the ground floor and between the existing building and the new extension is a service

Bedroom: Ample space for resident's own furniture: Bay window creates a sitting area and small window would allow view from bed, if bed were positioned at right angles to the position shown. Pendant light fitting is of a familiar domestic style.

Seating area around staff base is popular as this is where activity takes place.

block with kitchen, dining room, service stair and lift to the north side. The assisted bathroom and multi-sensory room are in the household for people with dementia and the latter is called the relaxation room as it is a modified version of the original concept. There is also storage, hairdresser, physiotherapy and art room to the south side. Within each household there is also a small kitchen, linen, sluice and housekeeper's store.

The staff base is opposite the entrance to the household for people with dementia. There is also a staff base for the nursing/residential accommodation on the first floor and is central to the entrance to the new building and existing buildings. Staff changing rooms and facilities are rooms in the roof of the new building.

Main offices are located in the existing building

Meals and laundry
The main dining room is for the nursing/residential care residents and dementia residents who are able and wish to dine there. Lunch and dinner are at set times but breakfast is taken in individual bedrooms.

In the household for people with dementia there is a separate dining room for those residents who prefer more intimate surroundings with a separate servery and hatchway where meals can be served safely.

Laundry, maintenance and plant rooms together with staff facilities are in the roof of the new extension.

Site context
Sloping suburban site on the north-west border of Greater London.

Philosophy of care
The client's intention is:
- *To enable our highly individual residents to live with dignity and freedom of choice amid surroundings that are physically and mentally comfortable.*
- *To preserve maximum independence we will help each person to choose, as far as possible, what level of care they need.*
- *To decide this in consultation with the individual, to respect their decisions and abide by them – intervening only where absolutely necessary in the interests of safety.*
- *A non-institutional environment is essential*
- *We may not always achieve this but we will try!*
- *Families are more relaxed when they realise their relatives are well cared for. This is a place which residents and families can be proud of.*

Philosophy expression in the building design

Generous space standards enable a high level of personal choice for residents, both in their own room and in the communal areas, which are arranged into many different spaces, large and small.

Wellbeing issues demand a good quality to private and public spaces: daylight, access to nature, views, materials, etc.

Circulation in the dementia wing is designed to avoid dead ends and provide a discreet level of observation throughout.

As the residents are all from the acting profession, theatricality is expressed in the form of a lot of display material: posters, portraits, etc and drama is expressed in some of the public spaces, notably the theatre foyer and main staircase.

Aspects of the building design that work well and which are worth repeating

In the household for people with dementia the internal courtyard brings daylight into the building, provides a secure space and glazing allows views across for discreet monitoring. The radial plan works well and allows residents to walk safely around the interior if inclement weather prevents them going outside.

Lower level external garden area is accessed via an alcove at each end of the corridors. Stepped terracing, planting and willow screen shields this area from the upper level walkway path without giving the feeling of being enclosed or overlooking.

Courtyard from corridor: Dining Room to foreground, handrail stops people from accidentally walking into the window. (Photo by David Wrightson.)

Courtyard with variety of planting and seats: Clerestorey lighting provides daylight to corridor space. (Photo by David Wrightson.)

Bedroom doors: There is no obvious distinction between these doors apart from the small room numbers and nameplates. Ornaments appear to have been fixed on as an afterthought, indicating that residents have difficulty in finding their own bedroom doors without this cue. The change of handrail material from timber to metal at corners provides a tactile and visual signal of a change in direction

Alcove at end of corridors and access to external goods area creates an 'event' and avoids a dead end situation. Access is possible to the outside, and the building and back inside via similar alcove at the other end. **Small frosted squares in the glass comply with building regulations for providing a visual manifestation of areas of glazing, but it is questionable if someone with poor eyesight would notice this.** Compare this with the courtyard corridor and handrail detail which is a more obvious and visual barrier.

Lower external gardens and stepped terracing: Variety of colours, textures and smells provide sensory stimulation. There is a walking path at first floor level above the top of the terracing.
(Photo by David Wrightson.)

The mix and size of spaces allow flexibility in use. Quiet private spaces are provided for staff and/or residents.

Other comments
The home is not registered for very challenging behaviour and was never conceived as accommodating that particular resident profile.

A larger dining room would have given greater flexibility for the other uses to which it has been put. Its popularity as a bar and meeting place have grown from the residents' own choice.

The client is genuinely pleased with the completed project as it is a good place to work, the new building complements the existing building and the design fits in with the philosophy of care.

AUTHOR'S COMMENT
Denville Hall is a home for actors (male and female) and provides nursing and residential care as well as dementia care. The existing building is from the Victorian era and there was an extension constructed in the 1960s which was demolished for this new building. The brief was to remodel and refurbish the existing building as well as design and construct the new extension.

There are several features designed which are specific to the resident group i.e. the acting profession. In the existing building there is a 'green room' and bar, where actors traditionally unwind after a performance. There is a small studio theatre, a double-height space foyer and grand staircase, which have all been carved out of the existing structure. Many residents like to make a grand entrance down the staircase! The foyer outside the auditorium is an important social space in theatres.

Additionally there is a library, card room and a drawing room. These are all accessible to the residents who live on the first floor and those residents from the household for people with dementia, who are able to use these spaces unaided. Those who require assistance can be accompanied by staff or relatives to entertainments and parties so they can take part in all activities.

The new building has bedrooms that all face outwards to either the stepped terrace garden or to the lawns; common spaces face into the central courtyard. Residents like to sit by the the staff desk at the entrance to the household as this is where activity is. This has been anticipated and space allowed for large comfortable chairs. The sitting room is mainly used to watch videos or special programmes. There is a separate dining room which is also used as a bar and lounge, and a quiet room plus the two conservatories at each end of a curved corridor.

Residents therefore have a choice of spaces, depending on their mood. These rooms all face the courtyard and full glazing allows views by staff into these rooms from the other side of the courtyard. A passageway allows access for the residents with dementia to the hairdressing, and arts and crafts room. This entrance, in common with all the entrances to the dementia wing are secured by a keypad. Those residents who can cope are given the code and come and go freely.

Residents can walk around the courtyard corridor and the bedroom corridor or outside. The internal corridor has clerestory (high level windows between roofs) lighting to maximise daylight and give a sense of drama to what would otherwise be a dull corridor. The two projecting wings end in a semi-external conservatory space which can be used as a quiet sitting alcove and also gives access to the lower garden area. Residents can therefore go outside and return back into the household at the other end. In the first floor residential and nursing accommodation there is the same arrangement, but the external route is through a wooded path.

The lower external space has stepped terracing with planting to reduce the height and maximise daylight and a willow screen at the top allows daylight to diffuse through without compromising privacy. At the lower level, externally and to the courtyard, the eaves heights and the use and detailing of materials gives a domestic scale in a contemporary manner.

The bedrooms are well-sized and have either a large bay window or a recessed bay with a planting area in front of the window. On the ground floor the glazing is full height, first floor the glazing starts at cill level and the bedrooms facing the lawn have a small balcony. The bedrooms on the 'radial' have sloping ceilings following the line of the roof. Furniture is provided by the home but residents are free to bring their own. Wardrobes are built in. En-suites have coloured tiles and contrast with the sanitary ware. Bedroom doors are all a timber veneer and some residents have their own items on the door for personalisation and to help with orientation.

Floor finishes are non-patterned carpets (vinyl to wet areas), plain pastel and neutral colours on walls and plain ceilings. Omitting heavy patterns helps to reduce confusion in people with dementia.

On both floors the room doors are recessed with a shelf display area. There is scope for residents to personalise this area as if it were a front porch, but this has not happened yet. The bedrooms to the first floor of the existing building vary in size and layout and are moulded around the existing structure.

The building presents a very domestic scale and proportion to the courtyard and the external areas facing the 'radial'. Facing the lawn and facing the entrance the appearance is more formal and appropriate for the size and scale of these external areas, and complements the Victorian gothic of the existing building. Passive stack ventilation is used and not traditional extract fans and these stacks are designed as 'chimneys' on the new building.

Denville Hall has successfully addressed the issue of providing a domestic environment for a specific user group and has achieved this by use of different spaces, use of daylight and by using traditional materials (brickwork, copper roofing, timber) in a contemporary manner. The finished result is a building exhibiting quality in design and quality of materials and providing a pleasant environment for the people who live there.

Ensuite: Contrast between tiling and sanitary ware and change in tiling colours reduce any institutional appearance. Worktop and inset sink allow for resting elbows while sitting at the washbasin and placing toiletries. Space underneath also allows for wheelchair access. Open shelves help people with impaired memory remember where objects are. The closed cupboard can be used for storing non-essential items

Eplehagen Bofelleskap

REASONS FOR SELECTION
➤ **Domestic and homely scale**
➤ **Generously-sized bedrooms**
➤ **Well-designed courtyard garden**
➤ **Daycentre on site (currently not in use)**

EPLEHAGEN BOFELLESSKAP
Tuneveien 21
1709
Sarpsborg
Norway

Contact for further information
Astrid Andersen, Norwegian Centre for Dementia
Research astrid.andersen@nordemens.no
ebt@sarpsborg.com

Owner Municipality of Sarpsborg

Website www.sarpsborg.com

Courtyard: Gravel surrounding tool shed acts as a deterrent to walking on this surface and is more subtle than erecting a fence. Granite setts on the path create a clear edging in a contrasting texture and colour.

Open since
2003

Architect
MVG arkitekter a/s

Resident profile
16 residents with dementia.

Number of residents
Two households of eight residents. Also within the building are a day centre and offices for the local municipality homecare workers.

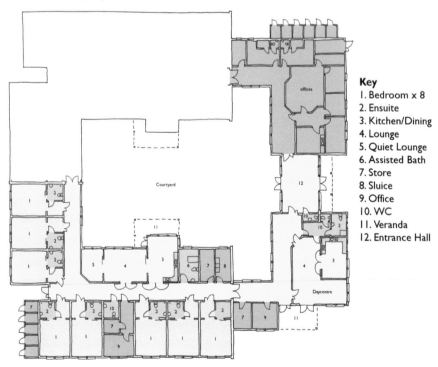

Key
1. Bedroom x 8
2. Ensuite
3. Kitchen/Dining
4. Lounge
5. Quiet Lounge
6. Assisted Bath
7. Store
8. Sluice
9. Office
10. WC
11. Veranda
12. Entrance Hall

Typical bedroom floor area
28.0sq.m plus 5.7sq.m en-suite: 33.7sq.m total

Floor area of each household
590sq.m

Building density
73.75sq.m /resident

Site area
2350sq.m

Site density
110.4sq.m / resident (not including daycare and office space)

Staffing
Unknown

Service and ancillary space
Each household has its own kitchen and a separate kitchen for preparing and cooking food that could present a hazard to residents e.g. boiling a pan of water. There is a utility/sluice room in each household. The staff base is a separate room in each household.

The day centre has its own kitchen and toilet facilities.

Meals and laundry
There is one secure kitchen where a part-time cook can undertake any hazardous cooking activities and this serves both households. Residents also take part in meal preparation, the extent of which will depend on their individual capabilities. All meals are eaten together by the residents as a family meal.

Laundry is undertaken by staff. Residents help with folding laundry only.

Site context
Flat suburban site in a small town to the east of the Oslo fjord.

Aspects of the building that work well and are worth repeating
- *Enclosed courtyard garden*
- *Path edging, use of gravel instead of fencing as a barrier, variety of textures, smells and colours to garden areas*
- *Generous bedroom sizes*
- *Second kitchen for potentially hazardous activities*
- *Domestic feel to lounge and dining areas*

Change in surfacing around old pump acts to 'warn' of this object and help avoid accidentally walking into it. The pump itself is a familiar object and is connected to the water supply and is used for watering plants.

Bedroom: Large enough to create a sitting area and a sleeping area. **Change in floor colour between this room, en-suite and corridor could be a problem. Rug would also be a problem in some countries because of potential trip hazard.** To the ensuite there are two doors, a hinged door to the hallway area and a sliding door to the living/bedroom area. Sliding doors are more common in Scandinavian countries than elsewhere.

Lounge with kitchen beyond: Polished timber flooring is found throughout Scandinavia and is common to almost all buildings. People have grown up with seeing glare and reflections. Opening to kitchen allows activity, sounds and smells to reach residents in the lounge.

Courtyard: Gravel surrounding pond acts as a deterrent to getting too close, eliminating the need for a fence. Variety of planting and rocks provide different colours and textures. Covered porch area allows residents to sit in shelter and enjoy the garden.

AUTHOR'S COMMENT

The outstanding feature of this home is the central courtyard garden. This is enclosed on three sides by the two residential households and on the fourth side by the building entrance and the corridor spaces for the offices and the daycentre. All communal spaces look into the courtyard and have access to the courtyard. All private bedrooms have a view to the outside. The daycentre has its own external space.

The principal access to each household is through the main building entrance, either side of which are the daycentre and offices and straight through the courtyard to the kitchen/dining to each household.

A continuous looped path allows residents to walk around the garden without any dead ends. The path is irregular-shaped, tarmac-finished and edged with stone setts to define the edges clearly. Whilst it has not been an issue at this home, at other homes with the same detail residents have been known to try and walk along the line of setts, not the path. Along the path are seats, an old water pump, planting beds, a water feature, tool shed and a flagpole, all of which are familiar garden objects.

Subtle barriers prevent residents from potential hazards. The edges of the path are clearly defined, the tool shed and pond are surrounded by gravel; this is uncomfortable for someone shuffling or for people with dementia to step on and they would not venture further if walking on this surface. The water pump is set in a radial pattern of stone setts, a feature in itself and a contrast to the surrounding tarmac. Someone walking and looking downwards could accidently walk into this pump but the setts provide a warning. All this is a more discreet method of ensuring residents' safety without resorting to fences and barriers.

There is a variety of colour and shapes in the planting for visual, smell and tactile stimulation.

The building enclosing the courtyard is typically Norwegian: single storey, pitched roof, timber cladding in the deep red colour typical of rural Scandinavian buildings. There is also a covered sitting area in each household facing the courtyard. External sun blinds also control solar gain and bring more life to the building.

Inside each household, the main entrance to the household is from the courtyard and through the dining/kitchen area. These are fitted with domestic-looking kitchen units. Two cupboards have glass fronts which are for the residents' use, the glazing allows residents to see the contents. The non-glazed cupboard doors are not for residents' use. There is a large dining table and residents tend to spend their time here because of the kitchen activity and external access.

There is a large opening from the kitchen/dining room into the main lounge area and from here there is also a second lounge which can be used as a quiet lounge or a TV room, depending on the resident's wishes. The dining room also has a fireplace, a familiar focal point to a domestic room.

The finishes to all three of these rooms is a timber floor and timber ceiling whilst walls are a neutral colour in the lounge areas but an active colour in the kitchen/dining space. Window cills are low to maximise views of planting beds by windows and the outside in general. Communal area furniture has been provided by the home and residents have their own furniture in their rooms.

The bedrooms themselves are very generous in size and more akin to a studio apartment. A sitting area as well as a sleeping area can be accommodated and with a resident's own furniture they will be more comfortable with more of their familiar furniture and objects about them. There is a separate hallway with built-in storage.

The en-suite has two doors, a swing door from the hallway and a sliding door from the main room area. A toilet off a hallway is a familiar domestic feature and allows residents easier access from outside their rooms. Opening the sliding door from within the room allows sight of the wc from the bed. Sliding doors are common in Scandinavia generally and would be more familiar to people here than perhaps in other countries. Throughout the home the colour of the en-suite and all toilet doors are a yellow tone to help residents with recognition.

Vinyl floor finishes are used throughout and many residents have placed rugs over the vinyl. **This is also quite common throughout Scandinavian homes but would be an issue elsewhere because of a potential trip hazard.** The en-suite has a coloured vinyl wallcovering which contrasts with the sanitaryware. A floor drain shower is installed with a full height shower screen. This can be easily removed at a later date if a resident cannot use this but it is a more domestic feature than an open shower.

Eplehagen Bofellesskap is of a very domestic scale and appearance with a superb courtyard garden. **The only downside is the institutional corridor spaces**, however, residents spend their time in the communal areas, outside, or in their rooms, not in corridors.

The corridor spaces are disappointing. They are very wide (2.5metre) with vinyl flooring and suspended tile ceiling and consequently there is an institutional feel to these areas. Seats and paintings have been placed here but these look lost in this large space.

➤ **The bedroom doors are not recessed, are all the same colour and have nameplates, with no other scope for personalisation or to help residents identify which door is their own.**

TV Lounge: Domestic size and scale create a comfortable space. The timber ceilings and timber floors in lounge areas helps distinguish these large spaces from corridors and bedrooms.

Sharehaven & Creekview at Evergreen

SHAREHAVEN & CREEKVIEW at EVERGREEN
Evergreen Retirement Community
(a free-standing not-for-profit organisation)
1130 North Westfield Street
Oshkosh
Wisconsin 54902
USA

Contact for further information
David Green, retired Chief Executive Officer
dgreen@evergreenoshkosh.com

Owner Free-standing not-for-profit corporation

Website www.evergreenoshkosh.com

Creekview: main entrance

Open since
Sharehaven: 1994.
Creekview north: 1997
Creekview south: 2004

Resident profile
20 residents with early to moderate dementia and low medical needs live at Sharehaven.
80 residents requiring long-term nursing care, some with dementia, live at Creekview North and Creekview South neighbourhoods.
There are also 175 independent living and assisted living residents in other residential options within the community.

Number of residents
Sharehaven: There are two households of ten residents all in single rooms
Creekview North: This neighbourhood is of four households of nine residents and each household has five single and two double rooms

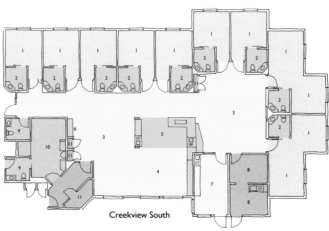

Creekview South

1. Bedroom
2. Ensuite
3. Lounge
4. Dining
5. Kitchen
6. Staff Base
7. Activity Room
Utility Room
9. WC
10. Bath
11. Store

Creekview South: This neighbourhood has four households of 11 residents and each household has seven single and two double rooms

Creekview South: lounge with dividing worktop partition which sub-divides the large space into smaller domestic-size areas. **Contrasting band in the carpeting could be perceived as a barrier but not all residents here have dementia so this may be less of an issue.**

Typical bedroom floor area
Sharehaven: 13.2sq.m (no en-suite)
Creekview North: Single room 10.5sq.m plus 3.6 sq.m en-suite: 14.1sq.m
                              Double room: 22sq.m plus 3.6sq.m en-suite: 25.6sq.m
Creekview South: Single room: 10.5sq.m plus 3.6 sq.m en-suite: 14.1sq.m
                              Double room: 22sq.m plus 3.6sq.m en-suite: 25.6sq.m

Floor area of each household
Sharehaven: 422.5sq.m
Creekview North: 221.5sq.m
Creekview South: 378.4 sq.m

Building density
Sharehaven: 49.1sq.m /resident
Creekview North: 61.5sq.m/ resident
Creekview South: 39.4sq.m/ resident
(these include the central neighbourhood areas)

Site area
35acres for the whole Evergreen community (141,642sq.m)

Staffing
All staff undertake multi-tasking roles.

Sharehaven: Two certified nursing assistant (CNA) staff for each household of ten residents during day and evenings and one CNA staff for each household at night.

3. Lounge
4. Kitchen/Dining
5. Activity
6. Staff Base
7. Utility Room
8. Bath
9. WC
10. Store
11. Neighbourhood Centre
12. Aviory
13. Office
14. Multi - purpose room
15.Garden

1. Bedroom
2. Bath
3. WC
4. Lounge
5. Dining
6. Kitchen
7. Formal Lounge
8. Store
9. Sun Room
10.Office
11. Garage
12. Entrance Hall
13. Garden
14. Staff Base
15. Utility Room

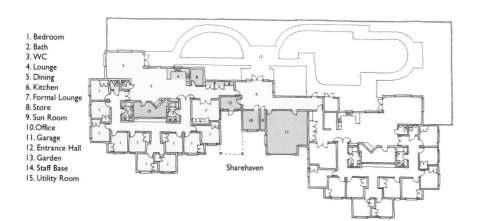

Sharehaven

Creekview North

Display cabinets are maintained by the local museum and are changed on a regular basis. This is a talking point and stimulates reminiscence for residents who can often directly relate to items on display.

Creekview North: One CNA staff for each household during days and evenings plus one floating CNA staff to assist in households with residents requiring more care.
Creekview South: One CNA staff for each household during days and evenings plus two floating CNA staff to assist in households with residents requiring more care.

A campus nurse for the whole retirement community is available 24 hours a day.

Service and ancillary space
Each Sharehaven household has a full residential kitchen, laundry facilities for all personal clothing and linens, two full baths (one with tub, one with shower), and two half-baths. The bedrooms in Sharehaven are not en-suite.

In both Creekview neighbourhoods, each household has a full residential kitchen, a utility room with laundry facilities for personal laundry, a spa for whirlpool baths, showers and hair care, and staff areas for medical records, medications, and supplies. Each bedroom has an en-suite with wc and washbasin and storage units for each resident for staff supplies.

Based on the experience with Creekview North, in Creekview South the kitchens were made much larger with more equipment, the utility rooms reorganised to provide greater separation of clean and soiled tasks, the spas increased in size and amenities to improve resident appeal and staff efficiency, and the staff areas for medical records and medications separated and dispursed around the household.

The staff base in each household is a built-in desk in an alcove at Sharehaven, and a recess space at Creekview. Because this has the appearance of a household desk this takes away any institititional associations with a 'nurse station'.

Meals and laundry
In ShareHaven, the residential kitchens, which are part of the living/dining areas, are used for preparation of breakfast plus entrée items for the other two meals (the main meals are prepared in a central kitchen and transported in bulk). As part of the activity programming, residents assist with meal preparation, serving and clean-up.

In all Creekview households, the residential kitchens are used for activities as well as for serving all meals. Food is delivered in bulk from the central kitchen and plated in the household for each resident. Residents have a choice of menu items and the quantity of food they wish to eat. Cutlery and crockery remains within each household, so set-up and clearing away can be a resident activity.

Site context
Evergreen is a not-for-profit continuing care retirement community. The campus is made

up of 29 separate buildings within a suburban neighbourhood; it integrates well into the suburban context of this small city.

Philosophy of care
Person–centred foundational statements of Evergreen Retirement Community:
Theological Rationale
As God's people, we are called to love others as God has loved us by:
- *Honoring our elders*
- *Caring for others in need*
- *Helping people use their God-given gifts and reach their potential*
- *Doing to others as we would have them do to us.*

Core Values
- *Preserve the uniqueness and recognise the potential of each individua.*
- *Exceed the expectations of beneficiarie.*
- *Nurture "family" relationships*
- *Encourage resident participation in decision-making*
- *Determine fees by cost and equity*
- *Share our knowledge of long-term care*
- *Commit to quality and excellence.*

Vision
The vision for the beneficiaries of Evergreen is to have the resources and support to pursue their aspirations and maximise their potential.

Mission
Based on Christian values, the mission of Evergreen is to provide beneficiaries of all faiths a continuum of options and services that anticipate and respond to their changing needs and desires, and to utilise skills and knowledge to serve community needs.

Philosophy expression in the building design
A residential domestic environment is created with familiar residential spaces provided and by having small groupings of individuals.

All households offer direct connections with the natural environment through spacious views and free access to secure garden areas.

Resident participation in normal activities of daily living is encouraged. All resident activities are within very short distances of each other which encourages walking and social involvement.

Creekview North bedroom: uplighting creates an even, glare free light.

Creekview north: neighbourhood centre with aviary: This space acts as a crossroads with residents, staff and visitors passing through. Whilst there are no views outside the rooflights, vaulted ceiling and even uplighting make for a bright space. The aviary is a source of sound, activity and stimulation; some residents just enjoy sitting and watching the birds.

The buildings support the provision of person-centred care by dispersing staff work areas and resources throughout residential living areas.

Aspects of the building design that work well and which are worth repeating

High vaulted ceilings in the common areas and the residents' own rooms of both Creekview buildings provide open and airy spaces and allow for indirect, glare free, inexpensive cove lighting.

Secure garden areas with access from each household provide the opportunity to be outside if a resident chooses to be outside.

Common and external areas are easily visible, allowing discreet monitoring of residents. Staff work areas are convenient for residents to interact with staff Household laundries for residents' personal items prevent lost clothing.

The neighbourhood centre between the Creekview clusters of four households provides space for large and small group activities, family interaction, informal gatherings, and simple people watching, diversions and watching the world go by.

Serving food onto a plate in front of each resident (rather than being presented with a tray of food) and having crockery and cutlery within each household makes setting meals and cleaning up important daily activities.

The roof spaces under scissor trusses accommodate building mechanical services. The avoidance of corridors with walls on both sides increases the usable space for people. Direct external access to utility/laundry rooms avoids transporting trolleys for soiled linens and trash through the household, which is not something normally seen in a house.

Creekview North: bedroom doors. Residents have gone further than the memory boxes to identify and personalise their doors by fixing their own decorations and names. **Handrail and dado rail are both of an identical finish and for some people it could be difficult to differentiate between the two**

Creekview South garden: Tinted concrete reduces glare on a sunny day. Fence is low enough to allow view out but planting and lack of rails to inside deter any urge to climb. **The gate should look like the rest of the fence to avoid any residents wanting to leave and 'explore'**

Other comments

In Creekview North the neighbourhood centre area contains an aviary but has no external windows. However, bright and even lighting makes this an open airy space.

Sharehaven and Creekview North have a parlour room which was intended to be used as a quiet room or for small gatherings. Due to lack of usage for these purposes, in Creekview South this room is utilised for activity resources. The 'parlour' is similar to the 'front room' traditionally common to UK and Australian houses and culture.

En-suite toilets or showers were not provided in Sharehaven because of the expectation that most residents would require some assistance with toileting and bathing and regular cleaning of ten toilets would be a significant additional task for the care staff who are responsible for all cleaning. Sharehaven is designed to feel like a ten-bedroom home (not ten apartments), and adding additional en-suite rooms would significantly increase building costs. State regulations do not require an en-suite toilet or shower, consequently many homes across the United States do not provide them.

AUTHOR'S COMMENT

Evergreen Retirement Community was founded in 1965 and has been evolving ever since with Sharehaven and Creekview being the latest developments. The key to the success of Evergreen is the person-centred approach to care, the buildings providing the environment and facilities to allow this care to be provided. Resident involvement in daily tasks is a key to their comfort and well-being.

Sharehaven has a comfortable domestic feel. The recessed staff base looks like part of the furniture and there is no barrier of a desk or worktop between staff sitting there and the residents. The cupboards here have hinges that self-close to lock, but close softly so there is no loud clatter of closing cupboard doors that may distract or upset residents.

The separation of Sharehaven living and dining areas is distinct yet still open plan and the kitchen is open and domestic. The bedroom corridor has to be windowless because of regulations requiring a tornado shelter. Providing bench seating allows residents to continue with activities if they have to wait here. Walking routes can be around this looped bedroom corridor or from lounge to garden, to sun-room and back into the household.

A central space between the two households of Sharehaven is used as a communal sitting area and also provides access to a secure garden area. The connecting link between the household provides indoor walking opportunities during inclement weather.

Each household in Creekview North is also of an intimate domestic scale with bedrooms opening onto the lounge/dining areas, and these spaces are bright and well-lit giving a feeling of spaciousness. Recessed doors and memory boxes personalise each doorway and help residents to identify their own rooms.

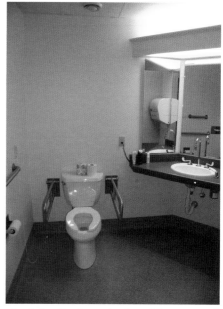

Sharehaven lounge: Change in ceiling level relieves the non-domestic appearing lay-in grid. Furniture, curtains, carpets are familiar to the resident group here. The size and scale of the space give an otherwise domestic feel.

The neighbourhood space between the households in Creekview North is well lit and spacious and works as a common space to gather, meet, sit or otherwise relax. The aviary serves as a focus and provides an activity and point of interest. This space is a circulation space which also acts as an active point of interest; if there were views to the outside this space could have the ambience of a village street or square.

This neighbourhood space serves several functions. Because it is the connecting link between the Creekview Building and the Manor Building as well as the Creekview North households, some residents like to watch and greet the traffic passing by as one would do from a front porch. It is also used for large group activities, small gatherings, parties, playing games or similar activities. The movable aviary is an activity for some residents, and is sometimes positioned as a focal point. While there are no views to the outside, this space still has some of the ambience of a village street or square.

The neighbourhood space between the Creekview South households has a very different design than Creekview North with many windows offering views of a garden on one side and through a porch on the other. The focal point is a large double-sided stone fireplace which is positioned to be a way-finding landmark from the Creekview Building entrance. Stylised porticos identify the entrances to a pair of households. The space is divided by the fireplace into areas for a variety of activities: music enjoyment, game playing, information gathering, fireplace watching, aviary observing, and children playing. The children's play equipment includes a two-story loft climbing frame which encourages active play that is fun for residents to watch as well as keeping grandchildren occupied!

The Creekview South design improved both from the Creekview North experience and from the challenges of increasing the household size from nine to eleven. This increase resulted from decreasing the number of double rooms in Manor View, the original 1967 nursing home. While the household layout of Creekview South is similar to Creekview North, the increase in the number of resident rooms resulted in a large open area at the end of each household. Staff have found this space valuable for group activities such as exercise and worship services. This reduces the need to use the dining area for purposes other than eating; using the same space for several different purposes can sometimes confuse residents with dementia. Another positive feature is an extended kitchen counter which is open above with a lower desk-height counter on the non-kitchen side. Residents can be involved in a variety of activities at the low counter while still visually connecting to the rest of the household, and staff can also discreetly monitor residents.

Creekview South has large display cabinets that are maintained by the local museum with historic displays that are changed periodically. This is very successful from the perspective of the local museum. It also provides a focal point and talking point for residents and families

In Creekview South, all resident rooms offer at least seven locations for the bed, thereby providing residents much control of the room arrangement, which is very important for residents to feel at home.

The Creekview South kitchen/dining and living areas are separated by an 'island' which contains administrative records and locked medication. With differences in ceiling heights and light fixtures this helps define the two areas.

The staff desks contain each household's charting and medical records and are located close to the household entry door and the connecting hall between households; this is a convenient location for staff to greet visitors, and is beneficial at nights when one staff looks after two households. The desks themselves have the appearance of familiar domestic furniture.

To help with orientation, each Creekview South household has a different colour scheme (see introduction) and furniture style which is based on the type of activities. Activities undertaken include gardening, arts and crafts, games and puzzles, and workshop. This approach to household differentiation was selected since these are the types of activities in which residents are likely to have an ongoing interest.

Between Creekview North and Creekview South is the main entrance to the Creekview Building which includes Creekview Center with a café, two therapeutic swimming pools (one warmer and one cooler), a therapy centre, an exercise equipment room, and an aerobic studio for group exercise.

In double rooms, each resident has the same amount of space as in a single room plus their own window. Couples can use one space as a bedroom and the other as a sitting room.

Evergreen's approach to person-centred care is reflected in these carefully planned and designed buildings. While the built environment is only one element of a person-centred environment, it is that element which initially is most evident to residents, families, visitors, and staff. It is also an important support to staff as they fulfill their roles using a person-centred approach.

Sharehaven: Dining/Kitchen with staff base on the right which appears to be part of the fitted domestic furniture. Files are kept in cupboards which are self-closing and self-locking but closing mechanism prevents slamming and avoids disruptive noise. **The ceiling is not very domestic but an attempt has been made to vary the surface. The change in flooring material and colour could be perceived as a step by the residents with dementia who live here.**

Fanny-Koti & Otto-Koti

REASONS FOR SELECTION

➤ **Domestic and homely design**
➤ **Popularity of double rooms**
➤ **Internal walking route**
➤ **Residents live as a big family**

FANNY KOTI & OTTO-KOTI
Kornetinkatu 1
33300
Tampere
Finland

Contact for further information
Paivi Karjalainen, Executive Director
sopimusvuori@sopimusvuori.fi

Owner Sopimusvuori foundation (non-profit)

Website www.sopimusvuori.fi

Rear Entrance: Cut out in wall and roof provide daylight to the sitting area overlooking alpine garden.

Open since
2002

Architect
Arkkitehtitoimisto Lasse Kosunen Oy, Tampere

Resident profile
20 residents with moderate to advanced dementia

Number of residents
Two households of ten residents: 20 resident total. There are two single rooms and four double rooms to each household.

Key
1. Double Bedroom x4
1A. Single Bedroom x2
2. Bathroom
3. Lounge
4. Kitchen/Dining
5. Sluice
6. Entrance Hall
7. Utility Room
8. Veranda
9. Sitting Alcove
10. WC
11. Sauna
12. Study
13. Store
14. Staff

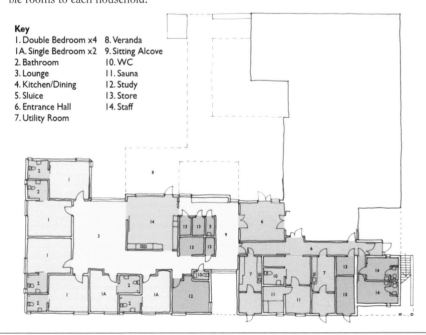

Typical bedroom floor area
Single room: 17.5sq.m plus 5.0sq.m en-suite; 22.5sq.m
Double room: 22sq.m plus 5.0sq.m en-suite: 27.0sq.m

Floor area of each household
395sq.m

Building density
39.5sq.m /resident

Site area
Unknown

Site density
Unknown

Staffing
Nine staff during the day with one overnight, between both households. All staff are fully trained. Many volunteers are also involved.

Service and ancillary space
Each household has its own kitchen and staff base which is also used as a meeting room for different group activities. Shared between both households are the sauna, utility rooms and staff changing.

There is storage within each household for wheelchairs, outdoor clothes and general storage. There are separate external stores and a bicycle shelter for staff.

Typically in most Finnish houses there is a sauna with shower and changing space and this is used every day.

Meals and laundry
Residents participate in planning, preparing and cleaning up after meals as far as they are able to and each household is self-contained and independent of the other. Even when the residents are no longer able to participate in any other way but through their senses of sight, taste and smell, every effort is made to include them in daily activities. The residents are encouraged to interact and help each other according to their abilities.

Cosy sitting rooms and other spaces are designed to support co-operation, togetherness and a home-like feeling. The sitting room and kitchen form the heart of the home surrounded by the residents' rooms which are mostly doubles and singles. The residents' rooms are furnished with their own furniture and textiles.

Kitchen/dining and lounge beyond: Tall ceiling, daylight and an 'active' terracotta colour on walls (see introduction). Kitchen units are typically domestic. Sliding door to lounge is usually left open. Ornaments on top of kitchen units are a nice homely touch. The analogue clock is also easier to read and more familiar than digital clocks.

Quiet sitting area: front door on left, staff and rear door on right. Change in wall and ceiling finishes and daylight from windows either side make this area very different from the main lounge. **The rug would not be permitted in many other countries as it presents a potential trip hazard, although rugs do soften an otherwise harsh floor finish.**

Mealtimes are set as this is important to a daily routine but there are no set wake-up or bed-times.

Doing things together gives the feeling of belonging to a group or family.

Cleaning is also done within the household between staff and residents on a weekly basis.

Site context
Sloping wooded site on the outskirts of the city of Tampere, central Finland.

Philosophy of care
The Sopimusvuori Foundation has 12 care homes for people with dementia:
All the care homes of Sopimusvuori Foundation apply the principles of the therapeutic community. Both residents and staff members wear their own clothes, not uniforms.

In all aspects of life in our homes the aim is to meet every member of the community with respect and as an individual. All residents have their own staff member who pays special attention to their well-being and care. In this way the residents' security has increased and the usual fear-induced reactions typical of people with dementia have decreased. This also has diminished the need for sedatives. The Foundation has its own training programme for staff members, too.

The atmosphere of mutual respect and trust is built in many ways. Human touch, holding an eye contact, and listening to other's feelings and needs are essential.

In each home some of the staff members have been trained in validation therapy. They use it in their work and help their colleagues become acquainted with it. It is used individually in everyday life and in weekly group meetings.

Remembering and memory has been methodically used to help residents to structure their sometimes chaotic world. The goal of these reminiscing groups is to let the residents enjoy being with each other, to relax and express their suppressed feelings.
Care homes are enriched by diverse training and previous work experience of the staff as well as by a commitment to their work. The director of each home is a registered nurse. This ensures medical assistance as soon as possible for the residents unable to communicate their needs verbally. The staff share all work and their special skills and strengths are used for the benefit of the community.

Bedroom: Sliding door to en-suite recessed in wall and low level handle. Sliding doors do not appear to be a problem in Scandanavia; **elsewhere people with dementia try and push or pull on sliding door.**

Residents can live in the nursing home until the end of their lives and they are taken care of until they die.

Philosophy expression in the building design
Internally and externally the building has the appearance of a typical Finnish house.

Spaces are large enough for all residents to go about their daily activities whilst still maintaining a domestic scale. There is space for residents to walk independently, quiet sitting areas and access to the garden areas.

In Finland it is common for children to share bedrooms then as teenagers to continue sharing bedrooms; a married couple share a bedroom, and therefore people have been used to sleeping with someone else in the same room. In old age to find one-self sleeping alone can be unfamiliar and consequently confusing and distressing. The double rooms are very popular for this reason. This is very much a cultural issue and almost unique to Finland. In most other countries single rooms are preferred by residents and their relatives.

Aspects of the building design that work well and which are worth repeating
The double bedrooms are very popular. Bedrooms opening off the lounge area are well liked; here residents still feel involved with the 'family' when in their rooms.

The layout of the household creates an internal route which allows for walking around via different spaces. This is important in the winter when the weather may be too severe to go outside.

Separate cupboards for outdoor clothes avoid snow and rain being brought into the household during the winter. Each resident has their own cupboard.

Underfloor heating and heated glass to kitchen windows: residents can lean against the glass and look outside. Low window cills allow views outside when sitting.

There is a special bedside system which alerts the staff if a resident gets out of bed during the night.

Other comments
The main entrance is through the garden and via gate. This gate tends to be locked for security so is little used. The back door faces the road and this is used as the front door more often by staff and families.

Vertical grabrail by the bedroom doors is difficult to see as it is in the same timber finish as the surrounding wall.

AUTHOR'S COMMENT
Otto-Koti and Fanny-Koti are the latest two homes of 12 homes built by the Sopimusvuori Foundation since 1991. Experiences and knowledge gained from the previous projects have all informed this design.

Lounge: Residents' own furniture and ornaments and domestic light fittings make this feel like a living room in any house. Bedrooms open directly off this space which aids orientation for those with impaired memory.

From their previous projects the popularity of double rooms is the most notable feature. This is very much a cultural phenomenon to Finland; in many other countries double rooms are non-existent or usually occupied by couples or two relatives. Residents here report that they feel safe if they know someone else is in the same room. Bedrooms opening off the lounge are well liked and a door recess with contrasting finishes aids orientation.

The other feature is the creation of an internal walking route around the household. Other Scandinavian homes have adopted the same idea because of the length and severity of the winters. A resident can walk from lounge area, along a short corridor with a lowered ceiling and a door in to the kitchen, through to the quiet sitting area with plenty of daylight, change in wall finishes and views to the alpine garden, back along a short corridor of coat cupboards, through the kitchen/dining area and its activity and access to the garden, and back into the lounge. Therefore there are opportunities for different routes within this layout, places to stop, different views and activities and not just a racetrack circuit around a corridor. From the lounge through to the quiet alcove there is a clear line of sight through the kitchen/dining area which assists with residents' orientation.

The use of room proportions and ceiling heights has been well designed. Larger areas such as the lounge and kitchen/dining have tall, sloping ceilings in a timber finish; corridor spaces, quiet areas and bedrooms have conventional flat ceilings at a lower height.

Rooflights to the lounge allow daylight to flood into the rear of the lounge. External recesses at the quiet alcove areas also allow daylight into these areas and these have been planted as alpine gardens, which add a point of interest.

Change of wall finish from paint on plaster to timber also adds interest and aids in orientation. The return corridor past the coat cupboards has staff only rooms on one side. The door finish and continuation of the handrails make these 'invisible' to the residents. There are low window cills in all these spaces maximising daylight and views out. In Scandinavia the winter days can be very short, and getting the most out of daylight is essential.

In other countries rugs would be seen as a ◄ potential trip hazard.

Vinyl flooring is used throughout but is softened by strategic placing of rugs. Residents are encouraged to bring their own furniture and they are also encouraged to have these in the common areas, if they want. Other furniture is acquired over a period of time. Therefore there is a mixture of styles, which makes for a more homelike environment – in your own home few people buy all their furniture at once, it is acquired over a period of time.

The kitchen/dining is the most used space; residents will stay here for most of the day because this is where activity is taking place. The tall ceilings, the colour of the walls, which

Ensuite: grab rail on wash basin which can also be reached from wc. Coloured tiles contrast with sanitary ware and external window allows natural daylight.

Bedroom door: Proportion of spaces aids orientation: high ceilings and daylight from rooflights to lounge, and to the kitchen/dining areas make them distinct from the lower ceilings of corridor spaces. Change in wall materials helps to define corners for people with poor eyesight. **However the door and vertical grab rail do not contrast sufficiently with the wall surrounds.**

is a brighter, more 'active' terracotta colour (although this may only be perceived as such by staff and families) a central dining table, door to the garden and the lack of any central work surfaces, all encourage residents to spend time here. The lounge tends to be used more for group meetings, watching television, reading or as a quieter space.

Bedrooms are well-sized with built-in storage in recesses or storage is behind doors. Ensuites have sliding doors that slide into the wall, maximising useable wall space. There is also an external window, green wall tiling contrasting with the white sanitary ware, built in storage and a very interesting washbasin detail with a built in grabrail. This is in reach of the wc and also allows a resident to steady themselves when using the washbasin.

> **As in other Scandinavian homes sliding doors are common and familiar, elsewhere people with dementia may try and push or pull a sliding door.**

Another interesting cultural issue is the sauna. There are no showers to the en-suite rooms and no bath; there is a single sauna and shower (in Finnish culture almost every house has a sauna which is traditionally used as the bathroom). The sauna here is used daily and is set out as a changing area with individual cubby holes, a shower area and the sauna room itself. The residents here will more than likely have always had a sauna throughout their lives as often as other cultures would have a bath or shower.

Both households share the garden area although each household has its own external covered sitting terrace area. A path travels as a loop down the slope to the bottom of the garden and back to the paved terrace area. There are planting beds by the building and a vegetable patch is also in use. Residents will plant, tend, harvest and eat the vegetables here. There are seating and planting to the rest of the garden but it is mostly grass and the boundaries are fenced with woods beyond.

The front door to both households is to the internal corner of the building and accessed via a gatehouse and across the garden area. The gatehouse also has a bicycle store for staff. The back door tends to be used more as the car park and the road is on this side.

The building appearance externally is like a typical Finnish house, single storey with timber cladding, timber windows and a mono-pitch roof.

Overall, both these households act and operate as two big families. All activities and chores are undertaken within the household and independent of the other household. The design and scale of the building creates the spaces for this to happen and answers many questions that arise from cultural and climate issues as well as those for elderly persons with dementia.

Gradmann Haus

GRADMANN HAUS
Fohrenbuehlstrasse 10
70569
Stuttgart-Kaltental
Germany

Contact for further information
Sibylle Heeg info@demenz-support.de sheeg@gmx.de

Owner Erich and Liselotte Gradmann Foundation

Website www.demenz-support.de

The two households are single storey. The connecting 'street' and sheltered housing apartments are on the left. External sunblinds have been lowered to some bedroom and courtyard windows.

Open since
2001

Architect
Sibylle Heeg, Social Design GmbH, Stuttgart with Herrmann & Bosch Architects

Resident profile
Two households of 12 residents with severe dementia, 12 day-care (moderate and severe dementia) and there are also 18 assisted living residents on the site.

Number of residents
24 residents with severe dementia

Typical bedroom floor area
14.7sq.m plus 4.2sq.m en-suite: 18.9sq.m total

Floor area of each household
710sq.m

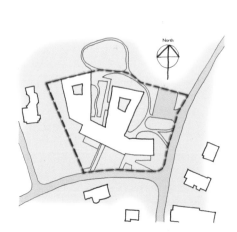

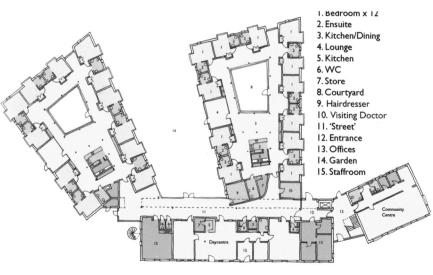

1. Bedroom x 12
2. Ensuite
3. Kitchen/Dining
4. Lounge
5. Kitchen
6. WC
7. Store
8. Courtyard
9. Hairdresser
10. Visiting Doctor
11. 'Street'
12. Entrance
13. Offices
14. Garden
15. Staffroom

Building density
54.1sq.m/resident (not including day-care or assisted living)

Site area
Approx. 4000sq.m

Site density
81.4sq.m /resident (including day-care and assisted living)

Staffing
There is a minimum of two staff per household of 12 residents on duty in the morning and three staff for both households in the afternoon.

Service and ancillary space
Each household has a small open kitchen area and a separate enclosed kitchen behind, where noisy or potentially hazardous or disrupting activities can be carried out. For example, the noise of a blender could be problematic.

Offices and administration are located in the main building. The staff base in each household is a desk cabinet located in the lounge and has a drop-down work surface that can be closed if the staff are called away.

Plant room and storage are located in the basement of the main building.

Meals and laundry
Hot meals are prepared off-site and are brought into each household kitchen. Cold meals are prepared by staff. The open plan kitchen allows for resident participation in preparing meals, drinks and snacks and open cupboards and glass fronted cabinet doors encourage this.

Laundry is done off-site.

Site context
On the edges of a residential area of Stuttgart with views across the Elsen valley towards forested areas

The 'street': Daylight, paved surfaces, exterior style windows make this an abstract, designed street. The grey wallcovering is an acoustic material to cut down on potential noise reverberation. On the blue wall are boards mounted with rugs and brushes; residents like to stand here and feel the different textures. To the right is the entrance to one of the households: the curve of the wall, texture of concrete and the colour (see introduction) identify this household from the other, which is a straight red wall and can be seen in the distance. Doors to each household are kept open to allow residents to walk freely between the two and along the 'street'.

Dining area in household: Open plan kitchen can be seen and kitchen activity can stimulate residents. Ample daylight comes from rooflights and the courtyard. Edging strips to tables clearly define the surface area. The overall interior and furniture is contemporary and contrasts with residents' own more traditional furniture. **There is nothing fundamentally different between the two households to assist a resident to identify immediately which household they are in.**

Philosophy of care

The Gradmann Foundation practise *a person-centred and respectful attitude to the residents as the basis of care. Residents are permitted to participate in the everyday group activities or simply observe if they wish, which gives them little sense of limitation regarding their physical and psychological needs.*

The concept for design is of 'milieu' or a whole environment. An approach that suits the characteristics of people with dementia in social, organisational, and physical terms which can in turn greatly contribute to the impaired person's quality of life.

Philosophy expression in the building design

The Gradmann House has been designed as a model for practising innovative approaches in dementia care and to implement a therapeutic milieu for people with dementia requires an environment responsive to their diverse and changing needs.

For example some people have a need to 'explore' and require a spacious, visually-stimulating, barrier-free environment which is secure and allows visual access and orientation. There are walking routes provided within each household, between households via the 'street' and also out into the garden areas.

Other people prefer a small-scale homelike environment which allows for personal contact with others. By having 12 residents to each household this provides the non-institutional domestic scale. Residents have the option of taking part in household activities such as housekeeping and voluntary involvement in such activities is an important part of the therapeutic approach.

Other residents require constant visual contact with others, providing a feeling of safety, while at the same time being able to withdraw for privacy.

Each bedroom has a bay window and six are en-suite, and six rooms share a shower-room between two rooms. The wc is located on a corner to allow a carer to stand either side if help is required and the wc can also be seen from the bed. Natural daylight to these areas also makes them more comfortable.

There is a deep recess to the bedroom doors from the corridor spaces, which acts as a front porch area. This is deep enough for furniture and provides a semi-private space yet visual contact can be maintained with common areas. Shared shower-rooms are also accessed from this porch area.

The corridor area in each house is a loop around an enclosed corridor and behind the enclosed kitchen area. Large windows allow views through the courtyard, aid orientation and provide daylight into the building.

Connecting the two households, the day-care, hairdresser room, offices and garden is the 'street'. This has rooflights and a coloured wall marks the entrances to each household.

Outdoor areas are accessible from the street and lounge areas and have a looped path and a raised planting area for activities such as growing herbs.

Aspects of the building design that work well and which are worth repeating

The street linking the ground floor spaces of the building together allows residents and staff to pass freely between each household and this space in itself can be used for a variety of activities.

Semi-private porch areas to each bedroom provide the opportunity for personalising this space with furniture, ornaments etc.

Toilet located to the corner of the en-suite allows staff to stand either side to assist a resident if necessary. This avoids the more common situation of the toilet located in the middle of a wall.

The Architecture department at the University of Stuttgart investigated the actual use of the building over a 24 hour period to see how residents take advantage of the choice to move freely and how life in the households influences the interaction between residents and staff. The analysis was carried out in relation to both space and person.

The conclusions drawn from this study were:
• A milieu that is favourable to people with dementia must be responsive to quite different needs which may change with the progression of the disease. When planning or remodelling dementia-friendly space, check if the concept allows for the whole spectrum of needs
• The needs of a person with moderate to severe dementia are not fully satisfied by living in a household with special dementia care and a dementia friendly spatial design. Absent-minded persons with dementia need individual care.

Concealed storage cupboards for storing linen or other items that residents do not have access to. **There is a lack of contrast between handrail and background making it difficult to see.**

Recessed area by bedrooms: Residents are encouraged to personalise with their own furniture and use this as a semi-public porch. A corridor loops around the courtyard and the bedroom doors. Windows around the courtyard allow residents to see across the household and to activity from their own porch. Natural daylight and ventilation are also brought into the building this way.

• Layouts that have a distinct spatial arrangement into households with private rooms, shared living and dining area and semi-private niches, combined with a generous space for moving about without dead-ends seem to suit all profiles of people with dementia. People with moderate to advanced dementia have a low sense of private territory. It may be the case that linear floor plans and larger living units may be equally suitable if offering diverse living areas and generous areas for moving around, allowing flexible shaping and building of groups.

Other comments
The separate lounge in each household is little used; residents spend their time in the dining area as this is where activity takes places. The internal courtyard is small and acts more as a lightwell but is another intimate, informal sitting area.

Bedrooms are furnished with residents' own furniture as are the door recesses. These tend to be more traditional looking furniture which contrasts with the contemporary furniture in communal areas and the modern interior design.

All wc and bathroom doors are red throughout. Wherever a resident is in the other household, or the street, they know a red door means a wc behind.

AUTHOR'S COMMENT
The Gradmann house exhibits careful and thorough thought and consideration from the overall concept down to the detail design.

Residents are allowed to visit freely the other household via the street. This space has the feel of an external space with much daylighting, external flooring materials and room windows facing this space look like external windows. By pulling areas out and lowering ceilings informal sitting areas are created. The door to the street from the main building entrance is cleverly disguised into the surrounding wall and is virtually invisible. The entrance to each household is a blue and red colour wash respectively, on an exposed concrete wall.

This whole area is an abstract modern architectural space which feels like a street without resorting to mock shopfronts or the like. Post-war modern architecture in Germany has been generally well-designed and built and has a greater acceptance by the population than in the UK and other countries.

The enclosed kitchen is also an innovative design idea. Noise can be a major handicap to someone with dementia so the option of noisy activities taking place in a different room is an advantage. A sliding door blends in with the wall so the room is unnoticed when the door is closed. An open plan kitchen area has no gate between kitchen and dining area and is therefore non-institutional. A breakfast bar also allows residents to sit and engage with any activity in the kitchen from the dining side. Rooflights allow more daylight into these areas

The large recessed porch areas by the doors allow residents to sit here without self-consciously walking to the lounge or dining area. Views through the courtyard let residents see others (and staff to see residents) and watch activity yet remain in their own space. This is the same as watching the world from your own porch or balcony at home.

The corner-mounted wc in the en-suites allows a carer either side if necessary, without having the wc in the middle of a long run of wall. Coloured wall tiling contrasts with white sanitary ware and grabrails and mosaic flooring makes a change from the usual uniform sheet flooring used elsewhere. The pattern of the floor here could be an issue for some people with dementia but no problems have been reported.

Ensuite: Locating the toilet in the corner creates space either side if staff need to help a resident. Often the toilet is seen in the middle of an expanse of wall. **The heavy pattern of the mosaic flooring could be confusing to some people.** Sanitaryware, toilet seat, handrails, flush control all contrast with the wall tiling.

The quality and workmanship of materials adds to the overall quality of the building. Timber panelling adds warmth to the common areas. Storage cupboards are concealed within walls and only a small keylock can be seen. Air handling is ducted via slots in the timber panelling, which are designed in and not stuck on grilles often seen elsewhere. Structural columns are also clad in timber.

Rubber flooring is used throughout the bedrooms and common areas but is softened in places with the use of rugs. **In other countries rugs would present a trip hazard and would not be allowed.** Ceilings are acoustic tiles in common areas and plain ceilings in bedrooms. Lighting is designed into the coving to give indirect lighting of 500lux.

Kitchen: There is no door or gate to the kitchen; residents can walk in here as they please. Meals are brought in and served from the kitchen. Worktop looks out to the dining area so no one here has their back turned to other people. The vertical screen shields the cooking hob and avoids the danger of someone accidently putting their hand on the hob. To the right is the enclosed kitchen where noisy or potentially hazardous activities can take place in here safely e.g. using a blender, the noise can be distressing.

Bedroom: bay window creates a sunny sitting area. Residents' own furniture and ornaments are very different from the contemporary interior and furniture in the communal areas

The secure garden can be accessed from the 'street' or the east lounge and allows for a looped path, seating areas and gardening activities. The open side of the garden faces a heavily wooded area.

As a model for dementia care the Gradmann house is an excellent example of careful and thorough thought, design and quality. Whilst the design is of an uncompromising modern and contemporary style, future residents who have grown up since the 1950s will be more familiar with this modern style and open plan living.

Hammond Care (Woy Woy)

REASONS FOR SELECTION

➤ **Large development designed as several domestic households**

➤ **Successful 'Y'-shaped floor layout with kitchen as focus for each household**

➤ **Service corridor spine**

➤ **Careful and thorough application of dementia design principles**

➤ **Garden is part of a walking route**

➤ **Latest development from Hammond Care, following success of previous developments**

HAMMOND CARE – WOY WOY
286 Railway Street
Woy Woy
New South Wales NSW 2256
Australia

Contact for further information
Stephen Judd, CEO Hammond Care
sjudd@hammond.com.au

Owner Hammond Care

Website www.hammond.com.au

View from road: Appearance is of several typical suburban houses and not of any institutional type of building.

Open since
May 2004

Architect
Allen Jack and Cottier, Surry Hills, NSW

Resident profile
Residents with dementia requiring low levels of care. Residents are generally mobile and ambulant.

Number of residents
Six groups of 14 residents; 84 total

Typical bedroom floor area
16.0sq.m plus 4.4sq.m en-suite: 20.4sq.m total

Floor area of each household
695sq.m

Building density
49.6sq.m per resident

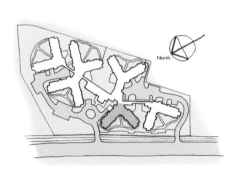

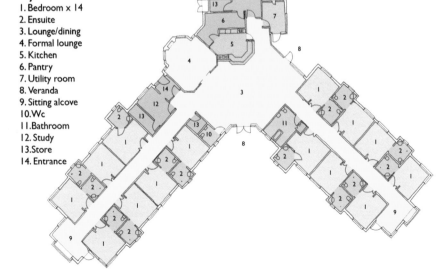

key
1. Bedroom x 14
2. Ensuite
3. Lounge/dining
4. Formal lounge
5. Kitchen
6. Pantry
7. Utility room
8. Veranda
9. Sitting alcove
10. Wc
11. Bathroom
12. Study
13. Store
14. Entrance

Site area
15,885sq.m

Site density
189sq.m per resident

Staffing
Two full-time registered nurses.
60 care staff in total, 30 of these specialise in providing dementia care.
Receptionist, maintenance, gardener, part-time laundry and cleaning staff for the central facilities.

Service and ancillary space
Each household has its own kitchen and pantry, laundry and study. There are staff and administration rooms in a central building which is linked to each household via a service corridor.

Meals and laundry
The kitchen is the focus for activity and daily routine within each household. Food preparation is one of the main daily activities and all meals are prepared, served and washed-up within each household, independently of the other households. Residents can be involved in meal preparation as far as they are able to, or choose to. The pantry is stocked via the service corridor.

All laundry is done within the utility room of each household, except for linen and soiled laundry, which is done elsewhere. There is a service hatch from the utility room to the service corridor for the transfer of laundry.

Site context
On the edges of a small town north of Sydney.

Worktop colours contrast with vertical surfaces and make the worktops clear. The lower worktop surface allows residents to sit and take part in kitchen activities. Louvred window to the formal lounge allows staff to monitor activity discreetly in there, or close the louvres if privacy is required. The view along the bedroom corridor can be seen from here and the ceiling fretwork detail foreshortens the appearance of a long corridor. To the rear of the kitchen is the pantry door; this is stocked via the service corridor and accessed from the kitchen. From inside the household the view is of food on shelves, like any other pantry. Cut off switches are out of sight around the corner.

Garden: All paths lead back into the household so there are no dead-ends. Gardening is a major activity for residents.

Lounge/dining/kitchen: lower worktop allows residents to sit and take part in kitchen activity and meal preparation. Kitchen is visible from all communal spaces in the household and allows for residents' orientation. Colours and objects (clock or picture frame) on walls help residents to orientate themselves as to which corridor their room is located in.
The polished floor could be perceived as being wet by some people with dementia.

Philosophy of care
Hammond Care are passionate about improving the quality of life for older people in need and recognising the intrinsic worth and value of every human being.

We promote the quality of life through dignity, independence, safety, resident improvement and family participation.

Philosophy expression in the building design
The building provides the opportunities, perception and access for inclusion for all aspects of daily living.

The open environment is legible and ensures all choices made by the resident are the right choices.

The independent front door for use by residents' families reinforces the idea of an independent house, not part of an institution.

Aspects of the building design that work well and which are worth repeating
Open kitchen and sitting areas create the impression of space without feeling empty. Activity, sounds and smells from the kitchen can provide stimulation for residents. For example, someone with impaired memory may forget about eating; the smell of food, the sounds of pots and pans, seeing the activity of cooking can act as a reminder about mealtimes.

Separate formal living room is used as a quiet room, for family visits, visiting doctor and is a very useful space. This is a 'front room' (or parlour in North America) traditionally used for entertaining visitors.

Visual access throughout the household common areas, ie lounge, dining, formal lounge, alcoves and bedroom corridors helps residents to orientate themselves if they can always see the kitchen. Staff can also discreetly monitor residents.

There are no dead ends, all routes lead back into the lounge/dining area.

The innovative service access to the pantry and utility room avoids institutional catering and linen trolleys being wheeled across the household.

Other comments
The staff take on a multi-task, total care role. i.e. cleaning, cooking and providing care. This is less disruptive to residents than having different personnel coming in and out of the house during the day.

AUTHOR'S COMMENT
This facility is the latest development of Hammond Care's homes and builds on the strengths of previous facilities at the Meadows (see Judd et al 1998), The Pines and Erina. Each household feels like its own self-contained home and not part of a larger complex.

The layout plan works very well, with the kitchen and seating alcoves visible from each bedroom door. This aids orientation for residents particularly if they should come out of their bedroom during the night. Staff are also able to monitor residents discreetly.

Garden access via the alcoves or lounge and garden paths leading back into the building ensure there are no dead ends and therefore, whichever direction a resident chooses, they will always return back into the house.

Careful thought has gone into service access. The view of the pantry from within the house is of food shelves, not of cut-off switches, which would not be present in an ordinary house. The pantry is stocked via the service corridor, catering quantities of food are not brought through the house. The doors to the service corridor from the common areas of each house are finished to blend in with the surrounding walls.

Likewise an access hatch from the service corridor to the utility room allows linen and large washing to be returned to the house from the central laundry. A large linen trolley is not usually seen in a typical house! Residents can help with their own small washing as an activity and there is an outside washing line for clothes drying.

The lowered kitchen worktops allow residents to take part in kitchen activities such as peeling vegetables but keep residents safely away from potential hazards such as hotplates. The kitchen door from the lounge is designed to open out and fix against a wall, effectively hiding it, but this door can be closed if required should a potentially hazardous activity be taking place in the kitchen. The kitchen acts as the focal point to the whole household.

The louvered opening between kitchen and formal lounge allows discreet surveillance by staff, or these can be closed off if privacy is required.

Gardens are used as an additional room, as the mild climate allows this to happen throughout the year. Gardening activities vary depending on levels of interests within each household.

Externally the scale is domestic with familiar materials and scale. From the road the premises appear to be a collection of houses; from each garden and from each bedroom window, the view is of, in effect, other houses. The service corridor when seen from the garden areas looks like the back wall to another house.

This domesticity is greatly helped by the fact that everything is single storey.

The multi-tasking staffing roles is also a key to the success of this home; the building allows this to take place with the maximum of ease for staff, to the benefit of the residents.

Hammond Care seek to push the boundaries of providing innovative care and the environments to allow this care to be delivered. This facility builds on and is a natural progression from the success of their previous schemes.

Formal lounge: In the tradition of a 'front room' for entertaining visitors and guests. Finishes, fixtures and fittings are of a front room, the louvers are to the kitchen.

Alcove at the end of bedroom corridor: From here residents can access the garden or sit on the window seat, see from where they came (i.e. they can see the kitchen at the other end of the corridor)

Heritage Woods

REASONS FOR SELECTION

➤ **Based on Tasmania ADARDS model***
➤ **Domestic cottage-like scale and appearance**
➤ **Large development split into small households**
➤ **Each household operates independently from others**

* (see Judd et al 1998)

HERITAGE WOODS
567 Goldstream Avenue
Victoria
British Columbia V9B 2W4
Canada

Contact for further information
Donna Prelypchan, Manager
dprelypchan@caphealth.org

Owner Vancouver Island Health Authority

Website www.viha.ca

Entrance to household: Raised planting beds let residents sit and work here. Armrests on chairs are essential for people with frailties to get in and out of chairs

Open since
March 1999

Architect
Jenson Daryl Jenson, Victoria, British Columbia

Resident profile
49 residents with dementia.
26 residents who are physically frail.

Number of residents
Three households of 12 residents with dementia and one household of 13 residents with dementia.

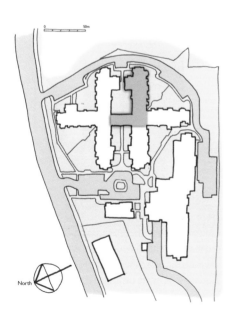

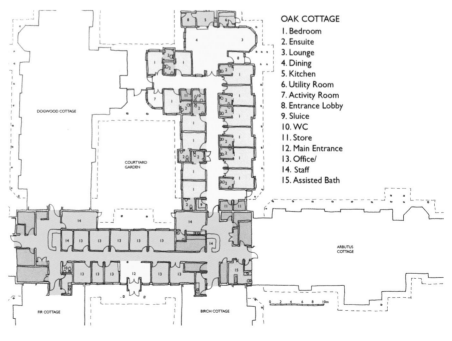

OAK COTTAGE
1. Bedroom
2. Ensuite
3. Lounge
4. Dining
5. Kitchen
6. Utility Room
7. Activity Room
8. Entrance Lobby
9. Sluice
10. WC
11. Store
12. Main Entrance
13. Office/
14. Staff
15. Assisted Bath

Two household of 13 residents who are physically frail.
75 residents total

Typical bedroom floor area
15.5sq.m plus 4.8sq.m ensuite: 20.3sq.m

Floor area of each household
539sq.m

Building density
45sq.m per resident

Site area
Approximately 6 acres (24,281sq.m)

Site density
323sq.m / resident

Staffing
One manager plus administration support.
Three staff are within each household during the day.
Two staff are in each household during the evening.
One registered nurse and three nursing assistants are on duty for all the households overnight.
Care assistants multi-task and provide care as well as the housekeeping tasks, meal preparation, etc.

Dining area: Reflections on polished floor could be perceived as being wet. Open view of the bedroom corridor helps residents with orientation and finding their way around. Furniture layout creates the impression of a formal space when compared to the informal lounge

Bedroom and en-suite: Toilet can be seen from bed which is important to people with impaired memory. Polished flooring could have perception problems as could the change in floor material from corridor to bedroom to en-suite. Sliding doors are generally left open.

Lounge: Carpets, curtains, traditional furniture, light fittings and ample daylight make for a familiar and comfortable space

Service and ancillary space

There is a central service core which contains the main entrance, offices, administration and staff facilities. Each household can be accessed from this central core via a hidden door. Each household has its own kitchen and utility room and is stocked from the adjoining building.

Meals and laundry

Breakfast and snacks are prepared within each household but other meals are brought in. Personal laundry can be undertaken within each household but large and soiled laundry is taken away.

Each household operates independently from the others.

Site context

Adjoining another care facility and set amongst woodland in a semi-rural area near Victoria, Vancouver Island.

Philosophy of care

"To provide a homelike environment that promotes resident participation in normal activities of daily living and affords opportunities for socialisation as well as privacy."

Philosophy expression in the building design

- *Each household is the residents' home, the staff are guests. Residents are encouraged to care for themselves, as they would in their own home*
- *The household as a cottage reinforces the residents' sense of living in a home-like environment. With loss of memory and sometimes confusion, those with dementia do better in a secure, quiet environment which is familiar and supportive*
- *The size and scale of each household enables small groups of residents to live together in a domestic environment to help promote social interaction and prevent the potential of over-stimulation which can occur in larger groups*
- *Each resident has their own space and is permitted to work within this space to make it their own e.g. decoration, furniture, personal mementos*

External garden areas are accessible and secure.

Aspects of the building design that work well and which are worth repeating

- *The ability to see the common areas and kitchen from the bedroom corridor helps the residents with orientation and allows discreet monitoring by staff*
- *An independent, but secure, front door to each household reinforces sense of independence, particularly for visiting families who can come and go as if they were visiting their relatives in their own home*
- *Having the service access from the rear of the household and the connecting corridor is efficient for staff in terms of time and effort of walking between households*

Bedroom corridor: Memory box for each bedroom is used to personalise each doorway and provide a cue for residents to identify their own door. Corridor is wide but well-proportioned. Textile wall covering is popular for residents to touch and provides tactile stimulation and also helps with orientation.

- *Separate activity room avoids potential confusion*
- *The domestic, cottage like appearance and scale is homely, comfortable and well liked by all concerned.*

Other comments
- *There is no separate, private space that could be used for recreational activities and for confidential meetings or discussions*
- *Medication cupboard and files are poorly located in a cupboard by the kitchen entrance*

AUTHOR'S COMMENT

Heritage Woods was the first of its kind in British Columbia, getting away from the institutional model and embracing the domestic model. Extensive research was undertaken, including visits to ADARDS in Hobart, Australia, (built 1991) which in itself was one of the first domestic models in the world. See Judd et al 1998 for further information on the ADARDS house.

The overall impression is of a west Canadian cottage and everything is very homelike and domestic in scale and appearance. Carpets in lounge and corridors, timber mouldings, domestic furniture, plain ceilings, houseplants all add to this. Bedrooms, dining and kitchen areas have vinyl flooring that looks like timber.

> Timber floors are common in Canada but the glare and reflections could be perceived as being wet by people with dementia.

> There is a lot of dark stained timber which gives a drab, rather than muted appearance, but this is a cosmetic issue which could be easily changed.

The communal lounge is a comfortable, well-proportioned space with a large bay window offering different views outside whilst allowing plenty of daylight inside. Traditional-looking furniture, curtains and light fittings all add to this. The dining area is more open with a timber effect floor, similar to the bedrooms with the same potential consequences. The open-plan arrangement allows for views out of both sides of the building and to vary direct sunlight over the day. This too can help residents with impaired memory; if the sun is shining into a certain room in the afternoon, this can help give an order to the day.

The kitchen is an 'ordinary' kitchen in size and appearance and with a back door as in any other house. The kitchen is a separate room with a door and large hatch opening which can be closed if necessary. The location of the files, records and medication in a cupboard adjacent to the kitchen door creates problems. However the absence of a staff base or nurse station overcomes any institutional associations as a 'nurse station' is not a space that would be found in peoples' own homes.

Kitchen: Typical domestic kitchen. **If a lighter timber stain were used throughout the interior would appear much brighter. The effect here is 'drab' rather than subdued.**

The utility room is also a familiar space to most houses and to the residents; the ability to undertake their own washing and hang washing out to dry is an important activity which allows residents to contribute towards the running of the household.

There is a separate activity room for painting, music or other activities. Anecdotal evidence from other homes shows that some residents can become confused if activities, such as painting, are carried out in the same space that is used for, say, eating. A separate activity space or room can overcome this problem.

The bedrooms are well-proportioned with doors recessed off the corridor with memory boxes by each door which helps residents to identify their own room. The wc in the en-suite can be clearly seen from the bed and a corner vanity unit makes the best use of space.

Externally the single storey, traditional timber detailing, timber fencing and a conventional, garden with seating, etc. all add to the domesticity.

A covered veranda running from the front door, adjoining the lounge, along the building and back inside via the 'back door' creates a wandering route. The mild, if wet, climate of Western Canada allows for external use of veranda and garden for most of the year.

Concealed doors to staff-only rooms are effectively 'hidden' to residents.

The central service core is similar to the ADARDS model and allows for staff to access each household discreetly and to travel between households, or to service rooms in the core very quickly. This is particularly important overnight. These access doors from the household site are painted as the surrounding walls and the dado rail continues across the door.

Heritage Woods has successfully interpreted and developed the model first started in Tasmania, Australia in 1991 for a larger number of residents overall yet has still maintained the domestic scale and household principles in the final design.

Highview Residences

REASONS FOR SELECTION

➤ Domestic and homelike scale and appearance

➤ Staff base is integrated into kitchen area

➤ Open plan common areas yet feel like separate rooms

➤ Assisted bathroom is a health spa

HIGHVIEW RESIDENCES
35 Capulet Walk
London
Ontario N6 3E6
Canada

Contact for further information
Ruth Constable, Operations Director tel (519) 657-4468
Cathy Chapin, Owner crchapin@acncanada.net

Owner Inspirit Residences

Website www.highviewresidences.com

Secure garden accessed from lounge: Looped path allows for walking and gazebo and different sitting areas and orientation. **White surface has a very harsh glare in bright sunlight.**

Open since
May 2004

Architect
Cornerstone Architecture, London, Ontario

Resident profile
Residents with early to mid stage dementia

Number of residents
Two households of 12 residents: 24 total

Typical bedroom floor area
13.7sq.m plus 4.5sq.m ensuite: 18.2sq.m

Floor area of each household
611sq.m

Building density
51sq.m / resident

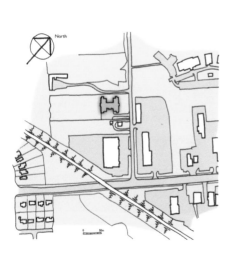

1. Bedroom
2. Ensuite
3. Lounge
4. Quiet Lounge
5. Dining
6. Kitchen
7. Spa
8. WC
9. Utility Room
10. Store
11. Staff
12. Office
13. Entrance Hall
14. Enclosed Porch

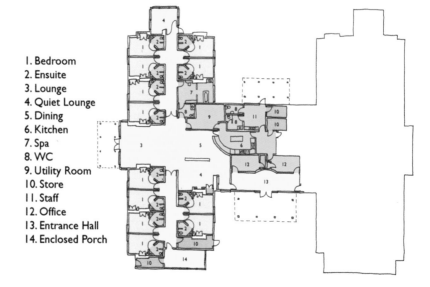

Site area
Approximately three acres (12,140sq.m)

Site density
505sq.m / resident currently. On completion of the second building on the site this will reduce to 253sq.m /resident.

Staffing
One manager. For each household there are two care staff during the day and one care staff overnight, one of whom is a registered nurse.
There are also part-time cook, maintenance and housekeeper

Service and ancillary space
There is a central service space for deliveries, storage and staff accommodation. There is a shared pantry between both kitchens and this opens into the kitchen so food deliveries do not have to come through the household.

Each household has its own utility room.

Staff base is located within the kitchen area to each household.

Meals and laundry
All meals are prepared in the each kitchen and residents help as far as possible within their own abilities and as regulations will allow.

Regulations do not allow residents to be directly involved with laundry except for folding dry items.

Site context
Flat suburban site on the edges of a residential area. London is a medium-sized city west of Toronto.

Lounge: Tall ceiling and daylight create a feeling of openness. Carpets and traditional furniture and a piano create a more formal space than the quiet lounge.

Communal areas: Kitchen on the right, the dining area is central, quiet lounge on left and main lounge beyond. Half-height partition and coffered ceiling helps to sub-divide the space as well as providing a shelf for houseplants. Uplighting provides glare-free lighting. Lowered kitchen worktop allows residents to be involved with activity in the kitchen.

Quiet Lounge: Typical 'parlour' as found in most North American houses.

Spa: Visiting hairdresser space in the foreground and assisted bathroom behind. The use of glass blocks, hanging plants and folding screen create the ambience of a spa.

Philosophy of care

Highview Motto: *To the glory of God alone*

Mission Statement: *Highview residences strive to provide a home where each individual receives supportive direction that draws upon their strengths, abilities and past interests. Providing opportunities through daily activities that respect and engage their passions help residents to experience daily successes.*

Philosophy expression in the building design

"The key qualities of home are realised at Highfield: domestic, warm and inviting; enabling people to engage in activities as they would in their own home. Highview has been designed to continue a homelike environment as the concept of care and to respect the dignity of each person living there.

The management commitment is:
* *To provide a nurturing community where residents feel valued and loved.*
* *To encourage, support and understand the individual needs of each resident so that experiencing a sense of accomplishment is a daily occurrence.*
* *To engage each resident in a variety of recreation activities, fun, outings, and therapeutic programs in the area of music and art.*

An important aspect is to settle the family into the home, not just the resident. Relations between staff and family are as important as staff and resident.

En-suite: poor contrast between sanitary ware, grabrails and wall but the inset washbasin contrasts well with the vanity top. This also provides a surface for toiletries, resting elbows if sitting at washbasin and space under allows for wheelchair access. **Glass block wall separates the shower but could be a hindrance for staff helping a resident in here.**

Aspects of the building design that work well and which are worth repeating
* *The bedroom and en-suite layout is very successful allowing the toilet to be seen from the bed and the en-suite door opening out 180degrees and able to be fastened against the wall.*
* *The spa/assisted bath/visiting hairdresser space is also very successful and has the ambience of a 'spa,' not an assisted bathroom. Whilst the residents may not understand the concept of a 'spa' itself, this is a very pleasant room to be in.*
* *Open plan common areas can be seen easily from the kitchen and staff base located in the kitchen.*
* *Resident-accessible cupboards in the kitchen do not have doors so residents can easily see what is there. Non-resident-accessible cupboards have locked doors.*
* *The enclosed veranda the end of the bedroom corridor and facing the front is very popular as residents can watch the world outside.*
* *The design has proved very effective in providing the type of care the management want to deliver. Each household is independent of the other.*

Bedroom corridor: Suspended ceiling and lighting is not very domestic. Wall lights give the option of varying the lighting. Skirting board clearly defines the wall/floor junction and handrail can be clearly seen.

Other comments
The meeting room, with access from the entrance hall and the office is used as a corridor
The glass block wall in the en-suite could impede staff if they are providing assistance to a resident in the en-suite.

AUTHOR'S COMMENT

The building is domestic in scale, each household entered from a central entrance hall. The entrance to each household is tucked away in a corner of the household so as not to be obvious to residents whose curiosity may present a danger should they wish to 'explore.'

The kitchen allows residents to engage in activities with its open plan layout. The staff can work at their desk and also talk with residents sitting at the breakfast bar. Open shelves within the kitchen are for resident-accessible items, avoiding the situation of residents forgetting what is kept in each cupboard and rummaging through with consequential frustration and stress. Non-accessible items are kept in locked cupboards. The staff desk looks like part of the kitchen units and is non-institutional. Confidential discussions or telephone calls are conducted in the office.

The half-height partition defines the circulation, dining and the quiet lounge area. A raised ceiling above the dining area adds interest and glare-free, cove lighting. The quiet lounge area acts as the traditional 'parlour' in most North American houses. The main lounge area has a raised ceiling and large windows giving a bright and airy space. The garden is accessed from this area.

The bedroom corridor crosses the central common areas and bedrooms are accessed from here. Different colours for each corridor aid orientation and the layout of the communal areas also help residents to orientate themselves as to which corridor their bedroom is located. Recessed doorways give a semi-private space for each resident.

The assisted bathroom/hairdresser room is very successful. The simple addition of a glass block wall, planting, and free-standing screens transform this space from a 'clinical' assisted bathroom space to a spa-like environment.

Residents furnish and decorate bedrooms themselves. There are no memory cabinets, nameplates or door numbers as this is considered to be institutional and not something that would be found in one's own house. The wc can be seen from the bed and glass block partition to the shower gives a touch of a hotel feel instead of a conventional curtain and rail.

A seating area at each end of the bedroom corridor provides for a quiet sitting area or a covered veranda. Insect mesh screens and a roof make this a secure semi-external space and is popular as residents can watch the world outside.

The garden area for each household has a pergola, a gazebo for sitting, water feature, bird table and looped walking paths with a variety of planting. Close boarded fencing is on the boundary with adjoining properties but the other boundaries are railings and chain link fencing which allows views out to the surrounding neighbourhood. Each household has direct access to its own garden.

There will be another home built on a site behind Highview Residences, completion expected to be November 2006.

Enclosed porch at other end of bedroom corridor: Views out to street made this more popular than the quiet lounge at the other end of the corridor. Insect screens to openings are common to this part of Canada and have been fitted here. This encloses the porch area securely with a familiar looking material.

➤ However the glass block could impede staff if assistance is required to help a resident in the en-suite.

De Hofstee

REASONS FOR SELECTION
➤ **Remodelling of hospital accommodation**
➤ **Internal corridor becomes a street**
➤ **Large multi-storey building**
➤ **Residents' freedom of movement**

DE HOFSTEE
President Rooseveltweg 22
3068TR
Rotterdam
Netherlands

Contact for further information
Bert van der Lende, Director Tel. (010) 222-9222
Wim Parent, CKKP Architects wparent@ckpp.nl

Owner Rijnmond Network Care Providers

Website www.verpleeghuisdehofstee.nl

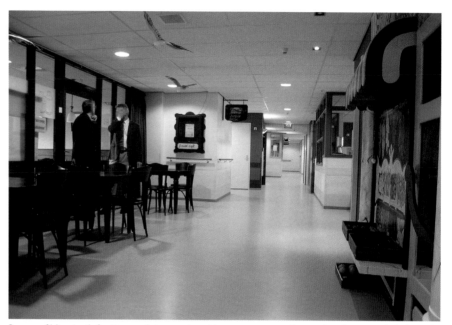

Brown café (see text), furniture and staggered corridors try to create an impression of space and of a 'street'. On the right is a replica market stall with real fruit, which also acts as an orientation device. **Large expanses of vinyl flooring, whilst avoiding any potential confusion with changes in colour or surface, does detract from this space.**

Open since
2004

Architect
CKKP Architecten, Rotterdam

Resident profile
143 residents with dementia.

Number of residents
There are seventeen households in total over six floors. Upper floors have:
One household of eight residents
One household of nine residents
One household of six residents
Double room for the provision of respite care
138 residents plus five respite care: 143 total
There is also a day-care centre on the site

1. Bedroom
2. WC
3. Bathroom/Showeroom
4. Lounge/Dining
5. Kitchen
6. Safe Kitchen
7. Utility Room
8. Guest Room
9. Sluice
10. Staff Room
11. Quiet Room
12. Cafe

Typical bedroom floor area
13.9sq.m

Floor area of each household
268.1sq.m

Building density
33.5sq.m per resident

Site area
Area of each floor: 1236sq.m

Staffing
17 management staff
156 care staff
15 treatment staff
10 part time ancillary staff

Service and ancillary space
There is a central administration and office area, restaurant, training rooms and conference facilities.

Service and sanitary rooms for each household are constructed as internal rooms, maximising external walls and windows for bedrooms and common spaces.

Meals and laundry
Each household prepares its own meals and undertakes its own laundry. There is a restaurant on site and residents have the option of dining there with their families.

Typical Bedroom: Bed is provided but residents' own furniture is used. **Vinyl flooring and suspended ceiling conflict with traditional furniture and ornaments.**

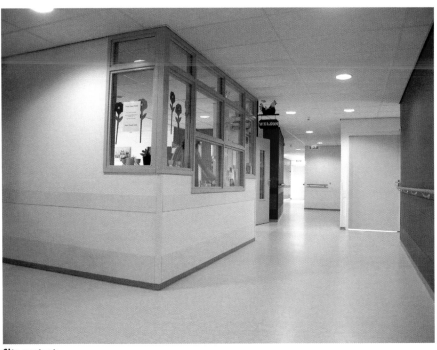

Kitchen window for each household looking into the main corridor/street area. Sign and motif (a chicken in this case) fixed perpendicular to the wall allows it to be seen from further down the corridor **although it may be too high up for most people. Kick plates, corner protection and dado rails are of an institutional appearance as are the suspended ceilings throughout.**

Site context

De Hofstee is an existing hospital building which has been remodelled and refurbished. The location is set back from a busy road in a suburb of Rotterdam.

Philosophy of care

Residents at the Hofstee receive care that is nursing treatment, as well as attention and respect as individuals. Positive attention is given to all matters and conditions that allow residents to live with their dementia as minimal change to their lives.

At the Hofstee living with dementia is worth living. Staff treat the residents as attentive, social, human beings. It is important for staff to have knowledge and insight into the aspects of dementia as well as the skills to lead the household and occupants to live peacefully together. Staff at the Hofstee receive full training to enable this care to be provided.

The Hofstee also offers recreational activities along with the provision of care in the form of a large number of associations. Family members and volunteers participate in these activities.

Philosophy expression in the building design

This philosophy of care is achieved by creating the right environment: Small-scale, ordinary, households of no more than nine residents. Surroundings are organised on this small scale because a homelike and secure environment is important to someone with dementia. Too large an interior environment can cause confusion to people with dementia.

The central 'street' on each floor breaks down the institutional corridor. The staggered walls and recesses and projections visually shorten the space along with borrowed light from the lounge areas. The secondary corridor within each household is on a domestic scale, as might be found in an apartment block. The service rooms act as a buffer between the street and bedrooms.

Each household has a common lounge area and the kitchen area has windows that look out on to the 'street'. Two of the lounge areas on each floor have access to a balcony.

Residents are free to visit other households and each household has different colour schemes (see introduction) to aid orientation and recognition. Each floor has either a multi-purpose room or a 'brown café' (a cross between a pub and a café which provides a key social function in the community). This provides a social centre as well as being a familiar part of Dutch everyday life.

Aspects of the building design that work well and which are worth repeating

- *Creating the lounge areas with large areas of glazing allows daylight to reach the central street area and the staggered walls break down the scale and long runs of corridor*

- *Household sizes of six to nine residents are more like living as a family than living as a large group of people*
- *Creating central service areas buffers the bedrooms from the street and maximises the external wall area. The red walls in the service areas identify that the doors here are to the toilet and bathrooms.*

Other comments
The existing building was stripped back to its structure and totally refitted.

AUTHOR'S COMMENT
Refurbishment of existing hospital or other institutional type of buildings is becoming more commonplace and De Hofstee is an example of attempting to break down the institutional model and create more intimate surroundings within an existing structure.

There is a lot of circulation space but having a hierarchy of street and private corridor works well. By not having straight walls, the scale of the corridor is broken down and the kitchen windows looking out into the 'street', borrowed daylight, a brown café and a fruit barrow (with real fruit) all give a sense of place. Varied ceiling heights and floor finishes would have helped this further but budget constraints did not allow for this.

Household sizes of between six and nine residents are like living as large families and residents tend to consider their housemates more like brothers and sisters as a consequence. There is a high staffing level throughout the whole building as a result of the small number of residents to each household.

Within each household the lounge areas are bright and the kitchen area looking into the street is a nice detail as well as enabling staff to monitor residents there discreetly. Residents can also see in to identify which household is theirs, or to make social contact with friends who may live in another household.

The bedroom corridors are like corridors in most apartment buildings and have access at the end into the street (for fire escape). Colour coding these walls (see introduction) allows residents to know that all red walls will have a toilet or bathroom behind the door.

Bedrooms have a washbasin but no en-suite, there are three wc to every eight resident household and two shower rooms for every eight residents. There is one bath located on each floor. Many care homes in the Netherlands do not have en-suites, the rationale being that few houses or flats have ensuite so people are used to leaving their bedroom to use the toilet or bathroom. In a household of six or nine this is also similar to sharing a bathroom with a family, rather than a large group of people.

As part of the daycare centre there will be a small 'pet zoo' with chickens, goats, etc. It is also intended to grow vegetables and other produce which will be sold to generate revenue.

With increasing constraints on budgets and use of land the refurbishment and remodelling of existing institutional buildings to current dementia design and practice concepts will become increasingly common. Hofstee applies these principles within the constraints of a tight budget and an existing building.

➤ Sliding doors can present issues with residents with impaired reasoning trying to push or pull a sliding door.

➤ Whilst residents can bring their own furniture, the hospital bed, vinyl floor and suspended ceilings in the bedrooms are still clinical in their appearance. Again budget constraints were an issue.

Corridor within household: Bedrooms on left and toilet/bathrooms on right. Colour helps with orientation (see introduction) **and although architraves and door handles contrast the sliding doors do not. The handle on the door looks like a handle you would 'pull' not slide.**

Kattrumpstullen

KATTRUMPSTULLEN
Roslagstullsbacken 7
S-114 21
Stockholm
Sweden

Contact for further information
Karin Magnusson, Home Care Director
Karin.magnusson@ostermalm.stockholm.se

Owner Ostermalm City Council

Website www.stockholm.se/templates/ template_236.asp_Q_number_E_56058_A_ category_E_24

Entrance: With balconies and folding glazed screens.

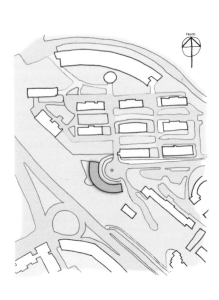

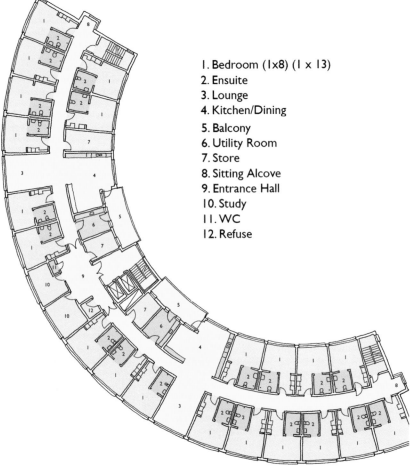

1. Bedroom (1x8) (1 x 13)
2. Ensuite
3. Lounge
4. Kitchen/Dining
5. Balcony
6. Utility Room
7. Store
8. Sitting Alcove
9. Entrance Hall
10. Study
11. WC
12. Refuse

Open since
2003

Architect
White Arkitekter AB

Resident profile
42 residents with dementia.
55 residents who are frail or have physical disabilities.

Number of residents
Five floors. Ground Floor has one 13 resident household. First to fourth floor has an eight resident and a 13 resident household to each floor.

Typical bedroom floor area
23.3sq.m and 24.2sq.m plus 6.5sq.m ensuite: 29.8sq.m and 30.7sq.m total.

Floor area of each household
Eight resident household: 424sq.m
13 resident household: 612sq.m
Common/service space to each floor: 137sq.m

Building density
60.5sq.m per resident

Site area
4662sq.m

Balcony: Folding glass screen is closed here. This screen allows balcony use all year and also avoids the risk of some people with dementia attempting to climb over the handrail. Access is from the kitchen/dining area or from the utility room. Chairs with arm rests are important for people with frailties for ease of standing up and sitting down.

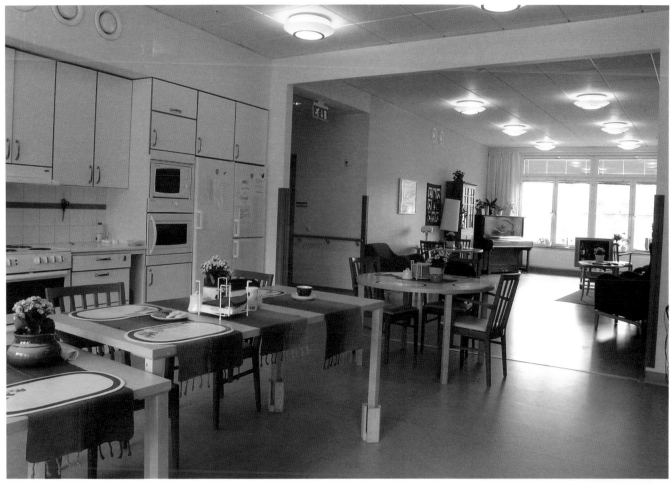

Kitchen/dining area: Open-plan between this area and lounge allows daylight on both sides and cross-ventilation and also breaks up the long length of corridors.

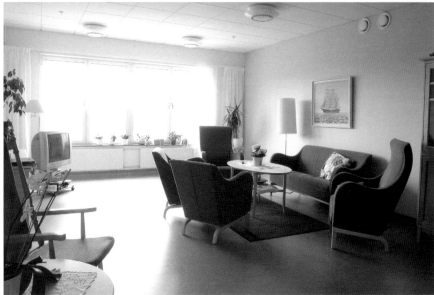

Lounge: large windows and low cill allow for plenty of daylight but **vinyl floor and suspended ceiling are not very domestic**. Contemporary furniture would be more familiar to people of around 70 years old or younger. **Glare from window reflections on a shiny floor could be an issue for some people with dementia.**

Site density
65sq.m per resident

Staffing
94 care staff in total
Six management and administration staff
One cleaner and one caretaker for the whole building

Service and ancillary space
Adjacent to the ground floor entrance there is a reception, library and café area. The lower

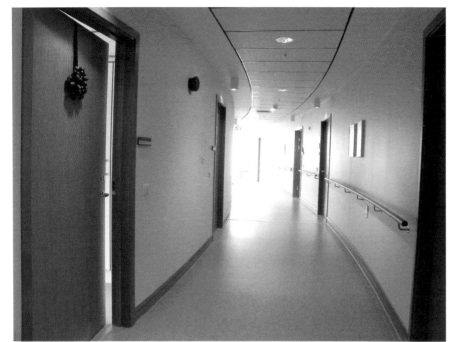

Corridor has an appearance more of a hotel corridor than an apartment building. Residents have fixed their own items to doors to help identify their own room, as there are **no other cues apart from a small nameplate**.

ground floor has a kitchen area, staff accommodation and a chapel. Each household has a kitchen/ dining area, utility room and store.

Central to each floor are the lift and stairs, staff base, laundry chute and medicine stores. Within the dining area of each household are further staff equipment storage and work surfaces.

Meals and laundry
All food is brought to site and reheated in the main kitchen and taken to the kitchen for each household. There is a small kitchenette to each room for making drinks; this can be disconnected from the electrical and water services if required.

Each household has a utility room for household washing with access to the balcony. There is a main laundry chute to the central circulation area on each floor.

Site context
An urban site on a rocky outcrop in central Stockholm adjacent to a housing estate and university buildings. Views from the garden area, lounges and bedrooms on the outside of the curved wall are over south-west Stockholm.

Philosophy of care
To provide a safe home for people for the rest of their lives. The residents' individual needs and correct levels of care are provided as well as social needs such as friendship, social events, and good meals.

The building is characterised by respect for the residents' integrity in a carefully designed and friendly environment. The elderly should be offered a personalised, homely environment where they can live for the rest of their lives and feel safe, just as in their own homes.

There is a general requirement in Swedish regulations for interiors of care homes to have the qualities of a private home and to have a domestic and warm atmosphere so that residents feel at home. These regulations were introduced in 1992.

Philosophy expression in the building design
- *The building form recognises that most residents have either a cognitive and/or physical disability with a decreased ability to orientate and often a distorted understanding of their surroundings. Room connections are easy to understand and room form clear. Each household has a separate identity and are separated by the central service/circulation spaces on each floor*
- *Social interaction is facilitated by common areas giving stimulation, change and choice*
- *Dual aspect views to the lounge, kitchen and dining areas provides daylight and choice of materials, colour, lighting and furniture provide individual character by:*

Bay window and seating alcove at end of corridors give views over the neighbourhood

Outdoor seating area: accessed from ground floor café and entrance lobby only.

- *A bay window as an informal sitting area at the end of each corridor*
- *Balconies which allow views over the entrance and street activity*
- *Curved corridor which mirrors the building form.*

The ground floor has a café which acts as a meeting point and also has access to the garden terrace area and views out over Stockholm. These areas are open, have lots of daylight and use natural materials. Residents, staff and families comment that they are comfortable with the building and believe that they have come to a good safe place.

Aspects of the building design that work well and which are worth repeating?
- *Large windows provide high levels of daylight*
- *Balconies can be enclosed with folding glass screens so they can be used in all weathers.*
- *Dual aspect lounge/dining areas break up the length of corridor and allow direct sunlight at different times of the day, which can help residents distinguish between morning and afternoon.*

Other comments
It is not possible to move beds out of bedrooms because bedroom doors are too narrow. This causes problems with very physically disabled residents and getting them into common areas.

There is no washbasin in the kitchen areas – a problem for residents sensitive to infections.

AUTHOR'S COMMENT
Kattrumpstullen is a modern building of a contemporary design on a spectacular urban site. The layout and appearance is of an apartment block or hotel. For people who lived all their lives in city apartment blocks this can be a more familiar environment than a suburban or rural house.

The design was selected through a competition. Kattrumpstullen has also been covered in Swedish press with a regard to improving design within care homes.

The simple curved building form is expressed internally by a curved corridor, which helps break up the visual effect of a long straight corridor. The length is further broken up by having the central lounge and kitchen/dining area. Bay windows at each end provide an informal sitting alcove and create an 'event' and avoid a dead-end, as well as allowing in daylight and providing additional views.

The corridors have a central suspended ceiling area for service access with plain ceiling to the perimeter; vinyl flooring throughout and walls are painted neutral. Bedroom doors are finished in timber veneer with downlighters above each door. In the households where residents with dementia live, the entrance doors to the household from the lift/stair lobby are glazed in obscured glass. This allows in daylight but prevents residents from wanting to leave the household and 'explore' elsewhere.

The lounge areas face the outside of the curved building with the views over the city and the afternoon sun; the kitchen/dining area has access to a balcony on the inside of the curve. The view to this side is of the entrance and street activity and this side of the building catches the morning sun. Sliding glass screens can be folded back in fine weather or closed allowing use of the balcony in wet or cold weather. Any issues of residents attempting to climb over a handrail or balustrading (which can occur with some people with dementia) can also be negated by closing the screens. The dual aspect allows daylight into these areas throughout the day.

The residents' own rooms are the size of a studio apartment with a separate hallway, living/sleeping and bathroom area. The bedrooms are generously-sized and proportioned with large windows. The built-in kitchenette allows tea and coffee to be made within each room, which is very useful for family and other visitors. By providing this, the residents can still maintain a degree of independence, by not having to go down to the kitchen.

There is generous built-in wardrobe and storage space. There is a sliding door to the en-suite which slides into the wall structure.

Linoleum flooring is used throughout but some residents have brought their own rugs for their own rooms.

Because residents can stay here until the end of their life there is also a chapel and temporary morgue on the lower ground floor.

The building entrance areas are open, spacious and of a contemporary design. There are views directly through this area and with the stripped timber floor, neutral and feature wall colours this makes an interesting and welcoming space. Residents can come here accompanied by their families and the local community can also use the facilities here.

The garden terrace area is accessed from these areas and in fine weather the café can open out to here, particularly with the afternoon/evening sun. There are views overlooking Stockholm and areas of planting, seating and a pergola for shade.

The entrance side has a more formal appearance and is in reality a traffic turning circle. A wide pedestrian area at the front of the building and conifer trees keep vehicle traffic at a distance from the building. The curved wall can act as a sun-trap and with the entrance, balconies, traffic and adjacent buildings the opportunity is here for activity, stimulation and communication with the community.

Kattrumpstullen is a modern building of contemporary design in an urban context. A large number of residents are accommodated in multi-storey living within a 'city living' style.

➤ Because all the bedroom doors look the same, residents have taken to fixing their own objects to help with orientation and identification.

➤ As with other Scandinavian facilities, sliding doors are generally more common in everyday life and are more familiar to people with dementia.

➤ Bedrooms have plain ceilings with ceiling-mounted hoists pre-fitted, which can be institutional, particularly if a resident does not require this equipment. Rugs are also popular in Scandinavian facilities, but regulations in other countries would prohibit their use because of a potential trip hazard.

Kingsway Court

REASONS FOR SELECTION

➤ **Part of a large retirement community**

➤ **Different floor layout plans for each household**

➤ **Central service spine**

➤ **Use of colour contrast and cueing**

➤ **Successful courtyard gardens**

There are many similarities to the Brightwater Care facility at Birralee, completed six years previously in 1998. Households of 20 residents are large and against the accepted practice of smaller, family sized, households. However, there are features at Kingsway Court that are worthy of further consideration.

KINGSWAY COURT
Madeley Care Facility
Kingsway Court
Countess Link
Madeley
Western Australia 6065
Australia

Contact for further information
welcome@brightwatergroup.com

Owner Brightwater Care Group

Website www.brightwatergroup.com

Exterior view is typical Western Australia domestic architecture including the profile metal roof.

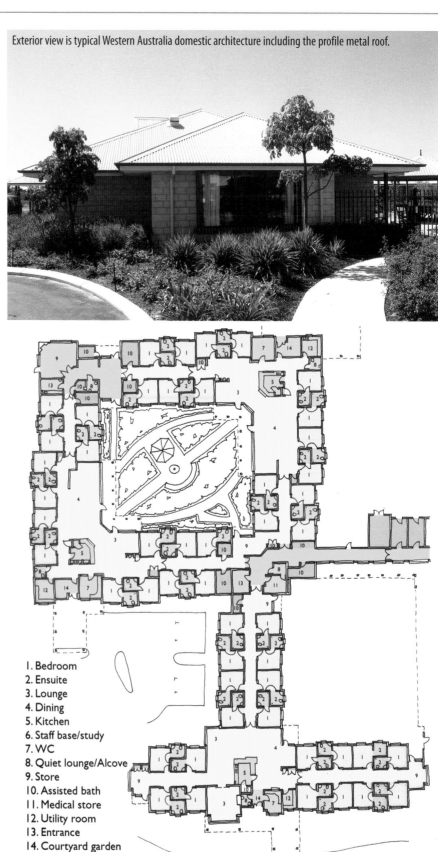

1. Bedroom
2. Ensuite
3. Lounge
4. Dining
5. Kitchen
6. Staff base/study
7. WC
8. Quiet lounge/Alcove
9. Store
10. Assisted bath
11. Medical store
12. Utility room
13. Entrance
14. Courtyard garden

Open since
June 2004

Architect
Brian J. Kidd in association with Kidd & Povey, Perth

Resident profile
60 residents requiring high-care
20 of these residents have severe dementia
20 of these residents require nursing or other care
20 of these residents are receiving respite care

50 residents requiring low-care
30 of these residents have moderate levels of dementia and 20 are receiving respite care

Number of residents
Four households of 20 residents and two households of 15 residents
110 residents total

Typical bedroom floor area
14.8sq.m plus 5.7sq.m en-suite: 20.5sq.m total

Floor area of each household
20 resident household: 830sq.m
15 resident household: 670sq.m

Building density
20 resident household: 41.5sq.m/ resident
15 resident household; 44.0sq.m/ resident

Lounge/dining/kitchen: Kitchen can be seen throughout the household and helps residents to orientate themselves within the household. Also from here the staff have views throughout household. The lowered worktop allows residents to be involved with kitchen activities. Cabinet above allows for personal ornaments to be displayed. Changes in ceiling levels and rooflights also help define spaces and break up large areas of ceiling.

Site area (of care facility only)
6900sq.m

Site density
62.0 sq.m/ resident

Staffing
There are staggered shifts throughout the day and the number of care assistants varies throughout the day.
For the high care:
Four care assistants from 7am-3pm
Two care assistants from 7am to 1pm
Three care assistants from 3pm to 8pm
Three care assistants from 3pm to 9pm
Overnight there is a registered nurse plus two or three care assistants
Low-care staffing numbers are unavailable

Service and ancillary space
Each household has its own kitchen. Utility rooms are spread throughout the building.

There is a central service core and connecting corridors to each household. The central service block contains a café, hairdresser, clubroom, offices and administration, allied health and staff facilities. There is also a large linen store and kitchen areas but these are now redundant as a cook/chill policy is used.

Deliveries are via the rear to the service core.

Meals and laundry
The kitchen in each household is for drinks and snacks and reheating food only. All meals

Lounge/dining with **different colour scheme (see introduction)** and joinery details to provide identity and distinction from other households. Differentiation through objects or details is preferred as ability to differentiate colours decreases with age.

are prepared off-site on a cook-chill basis. Laundry is contracted out but there are utility rooms located between the households for daily washing tasks.

Site context

Flat suburban site on the outskirts of Perth. The care facility is part of a retirement village that comprises 168 independent living dwellings plus a community centre

Philosophy of care

Brightwater Care Group state:

Statement of purpose: To enable well being

Values: people, caring, learning, innovation

Philosophy: Personhood

Quality statement: quality of care and services means achieving satisfaction for all (our) customers. Brightwater Care Group is committed to this concept, with every member of every team in the organisation empowered to contribute to the continuous improvement process.

Additionally, all Brightwater Services reflect the concept of personhood and a person- centred approach forms the umbrella theory under which all management, people services, training, care practices and support services will operate.

Philosophy expression in the building design

A domestic homelike environment allows the person-centred care approach to be realised. Residents are free to walk between the households and ease of access allows staff to support each other in delivering care.

Each household has its own personality and identity.

Aspects of the building design that work well and which are worth repeating

- *The different themes of colour and motifs in each household work well to orientate residents and staff to their location, as do the two different types of layout plan*
- *The courtyard gardens are successful and individual and provide variety and sun/shade for all throughout the day*
- *The clubhouse and café serves as a meeting point for the whole community and is very successful in that respect*
- *Front doors for each household allow families to visit without going via a central institutional reception area, as relatives would visit in any other home*
- *Internal en-suites have a high-level obscured glazed window to the corridor, which has a rooflight above, allowing borrowed daylight into the en-suite*

Bedroom corridor: Different pattern on door mouldings are a subtle tactile cue to residents' individual room. Window to en-suite allows borrowed light in from rooflight. There is a continuous carpet finish between corridor and bedrooms but a change in carpet signals end of household. Residents are free to walk between households. **Corner protections are not very domestic.** Name plate by door has a picture as an additional cue for residents to identify their own room.

- *Security is discreet and residents are still able to look out to the outside world*
- *Dementia care mapping highlighted changes such as de-cluttering and reorganising furniture within each household*
- *Staff facilities are considered to be excellent*

Other comments

None

AUTHOR'S COMMENT

This is a large building and uses the idea of the central kitchen/lounge/dining in 'L' and 'T' shape plan configurations joined together. The central communal spaces help residents' orientation from the bedroom corridors and also provide access to the courtyards.

There are many similarities to the Brightwater Care facility at Birralee, completed six years previously in 1998. However, there are features at Kingsway Court that are worthy of further examination.

Kingsway Court has households of 20 residents and these households are for residents requiring high levels of care. This is larger than other facilities featured in this book. The two households of 15 residents are for residents requiring lower levels of care and is closer to the accepted smaller size of household.

Residents are not confined to their own household, and are free to walk and visit the other households. Different colour schemes (see introduction) and the different motifs in the joinery and fretwork give each household its own identity and help with orientation and for residents to recognise where they are in the whole development.

Residents can use the service corridor to travel between households and to the central clubroom, café, etc. Coloured direction arrows to the doors aid in wayfinding. The household where residents with severe dementia live does not have this open door policy.

Bedroom doors have different moulding patterns on the door panels, providing a subtle, tactile orientation and recognition device, **although this may be too subtle for some people**.

Different floor layouts in an 'L' or 'T' shape also help with orientation, add interest and variety, **although the change in layout may not be as obvious to some people as the different layouts at Birralee.**

Independent front doors to each household are very popular; families are given their own key

Front door and study: Families have a key and can visit as and when they wish. Study is a common household room — a nurse station is not. Joinery details also help to distinguish each household from other households

and can come and go as they wish, as they could if visiting relatives in their own home. The formal lounge is used as a quiet room, family room and informal meeting space and has the appearance of a traditional front room, traditionally not used on a daily basis but only used for visitors. As at Birralee, Kingsway Court continues this tradition.

The kitchen is located as the focal point to all the households and has views over all communal lounge, dining, corridor and garden areas. With the kitchen visible from all the communal areas this helps residents to orientate themselves if they can always see the kitchen. This is especially helpful if a resident leaves their bedroom at night. Staff can also discreetly monitor residents.

Spaces, internally and externally, are domestic and of an intimate scale and appearance is of familiar materials and shapes. Varied ceiling heights add interest and break up large areas of surface.

There are some nice features to the bedroom corridors. A window from each en-suite to the corridor adjacent to a rooflight allows for borrowed daylight to reach the en-suite so it does not feel like a totally internal room. There is a continuous carpet finish from corridor to bedroom but a change in carpet between the household and the service corridor indicates the end of the household. Name plates by each bedroom door have a picture which provides an additional cue for residents to recognise their own room.

Most houses do not have a nurse station as such but do have a study. The staff base is therefore referred to as the 'study' and domestic-looking windows allow staff to monitor residents discreetly. The location by the front door also helps to monitor visitors.

There are no dead ends; all corridors end in an alcove with access to the courtyard gardens. The gardens are well-established and well-maintained providing open, shaded, sitting or active opportunities for all the residents with a wide variety of colour, textures and smells for stimulation.

Kingsway Court takes the successful model developed for the same owner at Birralee and progresses this for a larger building with a different resident profile.

Lemon tree: familiar to residents here, colour, touch, can be safely picked, handled and eaten.

Courtyard garden: variety in planting with variety in colour, size, texture. There are walking paths around the focal point of a gazebo, fountain and bench seating and a seating wall. The gazebo helps to orientate residents and the garden.

Martin Luther Home

MARTIN LUTHER HOME
67 Mount View Road
The Basin
Boronia
Victoria 3154
Australia

Contact for further information
Joan vanBaggo, Director of Nursing
Joan.vanbaggo@martinlutherhomes.com.au

Owner German Lutheran Church, East Melbourne

Website www.martinlutherhomes.com.au

Entrance with canopy by car drop off and landmark tower. Railings are to secure garden but allow views out. In Australia secure fencing like this is common in order to keep wildlife pests away from buildings.

Open since
Households for people with dementia were completed 2000 and extended 2003

Architect
KLCK Woodhead International, Melbourne

Resident profile
30 residents with dementia
30 residents requiring nursing care
There are also 28 residents requiring low care and 47 independent living units on the site

Number of residents
Three households of ten residents with dementia

Typical bedroom floor area
14.2sq.m plus 4.0sq.m ensuite: 18.2sq.m total

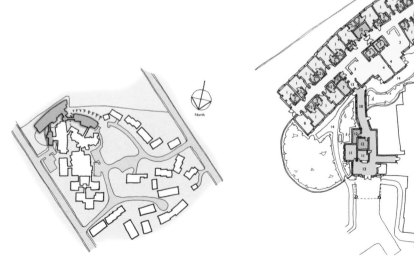

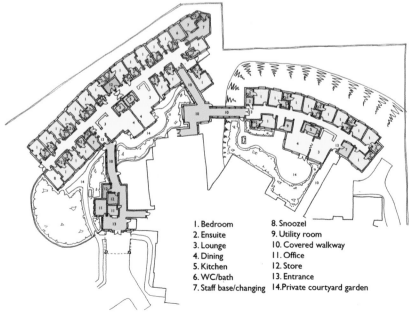

1. Bedroom	8. Snoozel
2. Ensuite	9. Utility room
3. Lounge	10. Covered walkway
4. Dining	11. Office
5. Kitchen	12. Store
6. WC/bath	13. Entrance
7. Staff base/changing	14. Private courtyard garden

Floor area of each household
398sq.m for each of the two adjoining dementia specific houses
418sq.m for the separate house

Building density
39.8sq.m per resident for the two adjoining dementia specific houses
41.8sq.m per resident for the separate house

Site area
2670sq.m for the households and gardens for the residents with dementia only.

Site density
89.0sq.m per resident

Staffing
In total there are:
Seven management staff plus 80 care staff in total
During the day there is a staff:resident ratio of 1 to 5 at peak times, 1 to 7.5 ratio at off-peak
times. Two staff are on duty to the dementia specific households overnight.

There is a total of 35 other staff: contract cleaners, maintenance, gardener. Cleaning is contracted out.

Service and ancillary space
Each household has a small kitchen. This is designed as an alcove off the dining area and has a
half-height gate. There is a main kitchen that services the households for residents with dementia and the households for residents requiring nursing care, with their meals. All laundry is contracted out except for personal laundry items.

Meals and laundry
Breakfast and lunch is prepared within each house but the main meal is at noon and is prepared
in the central kitchen.

There is a small washing machine in one of the dementia specific households for tea towels and
other 'activity' washing.

Site context
Sloping suburban site on the eastern edges of Melbourne.

Philosophy of care
Mission statement: To provide high quality services predominantly, but not exclusively, to the

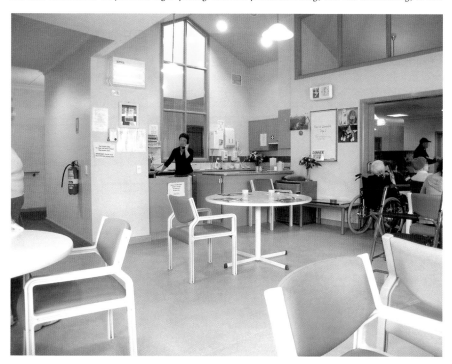

Kitchen/dining areas adjacent to lounge: Semi-
open plan allows sounds and activity from the kitchen
to stimulate residents. Half-height gate can discreetly
keep residents away if necessary. Change from carpet
to vinyl flooring is of the same tone and not too great a
contrast. Tall glazed screen allows daylight via
rooflights to corridor to enter kitchen. Openable screen
between households allows for larger group activities.

Lounge: Half-height partition with built in bookshelves and recess for settee sub-divides the sitting space for circulation, provides a secure 'back' to sit against and a shelf for ornaments. All toilet doors are green and have a picture of a toilet (see text) offering two cues. Hanging pendant light fittings are generally more familiar than recessed light fittings.

German speaking community within a Lutheran Christian environment which is designed to meet the spiritual, social, physical, emotional and psychological needs of each individual resident in a non-discriminatory manner to maintain dignity, self-esteem and personal well being.

Vision statement: For Martin Luther Homes at Boronia to be at the forefront of, and a leader in, the provision of high quality professional aged care services for the German speaking community, and the broader community sector, with an emphasis on spiritual care for its resident as well as professional support and training for its staff at all levels.

Philosophy expression in the building design
The building allows quality care for residents to be provided and the staff are able to be flexible and respond to residents changing needs. Staff are able to care for residents in a restraint-free environment.

In making the building as homelike as possible, the management consider this to be a success.

Aspects of the building design that work well and which are worth repeating
- *Colour cueing works well: all toilet doors are green and contrast with the surrounding walls. There is also a picture of a toilet so there are multiple cues.*
- *Clerestory lighting to the corridors and especially behind the kitchen allows daylight to reach into the kitchen and the circulation space behind. Viewing openings to the kitchen allow residents to see into the kitchen areas and also allow discreet monitoring by staff into the circulation areas.*
- *Courtyard areas are of an intimate size and scale.*

Other comments
Some of the ramped walkways are quite steep for heavy trolleys and travel distances for staff are quite long and inefficient. However, this is a consequence of the site constraints.

The bay windows in the dining area do not open; ventilation is achieved by opening the doors to the garden, which creates draughts. The enclosed walkways can also get very hot in summer.

AUTHOR'S COMMENT
The overall site has been developed over many years leaving an awkward plot of land at the top of the site, on a steep slope, and sandwiched between existing buildings and the site boundary for the accommodation for people with dementia.

This has necessitated the enclosed ramped ◀ **walkways and the fact that two of the households can only be accessed via other households.**

The separate entrance building works well as a focal point with its porch, tower and weather vane and has a welcoming relaxed feel to it. This acts as a landmark and residents in the garden areas can use this for orientation.

Access into each house is discreet, preventing residents wanting to get through this door and outside the household. Access to courtyard garden areas is via the bay windows to the dining area. Each household is connected to the central service block and entrance via covered glazed walkways.

The lounge areas are of a cosy intimate size and the half-height partitions walls serve to separate circulation space from the sitting space as well as creating bookshelves, a shelf for ornaments or plants and small sitting alcoves for furniture. The change in ceiling height to the dining area from the lounge also helps to differentiate these spaces. In one of the households the dining area has the higher ceiling, and this appears to work slightly better than having a taller space for the lounge.

With the kitchen designed as an alcove this keeps an open plan feel but by closing the small gate the kitchen can still be used as a secure space. Clerestory lighting brings daylight into the kitchen and circulation space behind which lifts the general atmosphere.

Cueing works well, all toilet doors are a green colour which contrasts with the walls and have a picture of a toilet on the door providing multiple cues for residents with impaired reasoning. The residents' bedroom doors have different patterns and colours (see introduction) to the mouldings which are also multiple cues to help residents to identify their own room. In my view green is also a colour associated with 'go' and 'safe'. Individual bedroom doors have different pattern panelling and panels are highlighted in different colours.

There is a single multi-sensory room which tends to be used more for activities than its original intention of a therapeutic calming space. Agitated residents appear to prefer being in their own room, surrounded by their own familiar possessions, rather than a multi-sensory room.

The end of the bedroom corridor to the east of the building terminates in a glazed door at present. This is a dead-end and some residents might try to open this door to explore beyond, and get frustrated when finding the door is locked. However this is a temporary situation as there are plans to extend into the open area of land here and this door will be a connecting door in the future.

Secure courtyard gardens separate the individual buildings and are well-planted and maintained creating an intimate feel. There is not much space between the buildings but the planting helps maintain a degree of privacy to bedroom windows. There is a bus-stop complete with shelter and timetable which is used by the residents to reminisce.

The residents are of German origin and whilst they have spoken English when they have been living in Australia, many of them have reverted back to speaking German as their first language or changing languages mid-sentence! The staff are also German speaking and this overcomes any potential communication problems.

The Martin Luther home makes the best use of an awkward site and has some nice details particularly in the use of bringing daylight into the building, the half-height partition screens and the multiple cues on doors.

Bedroom doors in different mouldings and colours offer multiple cues to identify residents' individual rooms. Carpets continue into bedrooms from the corridor. Glazed doors to the end are short-term; there will be another household built there. The contrast between colour and the door is more important than the colour itself.

Courtyard garden: Bus-stop with seat and timetable is used by residents to reminisce. There is also a variety of colours and textures in planting

Opri Ja Oleski

OPRI JA OLESKI
Pitkakallionkuja 1
02170
Espoo
Finland

Contact for further information
Taina Semi, Executive manager
opri.oleski@pp.inet.fi

Owner Opri ja Oleski Oy (private company). The municipality of Espoo have first option on the selection of residents, paying individuals are on a waiting list.

Website www.oprijaoleski.fi

External appearance is of a typical Finnish house, nothing to indicate any special needs of the people who live there.

Open since
2000

Architect
Tero Seppanen and Pekka Salminen

Resident profile
13 residents with moderate to advanced dementia plus two respite care residents

Number of residents
One household of 15 residents.

Typical bedroom floor area
12.0sq.m

Floor area of each household
500sq.m

Building density
33sq.m/ resident

Site area
1400sq.m

Site density
93sq.m /resident

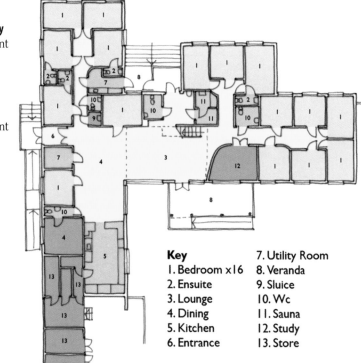

Key
1. Bedroom x16
2. Ensuite
3. Lounge
4. Dining
5. Kitchen
6. Entrance
7. Utility Room
8. Veranda
9. Sluice
10. Wc
11. Sauna
12. Study
13. Store

Staffing

Two nurses plus between one auxiliary nurse, five visiting nurses, one gerontologist. Also there is a cook, cleaner and a caretaker.

Service and ancillary space

The kitchen is a 'farmhouse'-style kitchen and is open to the dining area with wicker gates allowing the kitchen to become more secure as required. There is a separate laundry room and outdoor drying area. The staff base is a separate room located next to the lounge.

Typically of Finnish homes, there is a sauna with shower and changing area and this is used on a daily basis. There are internal and external store areas. Staff rooms and facilities are on the first floor.

Meals and laundry

Residents are involved with meal preparation and cooking but access to the kitchen can be restricted if required, depending on a residents' capabilities. Regular community meetings with the residents plan meals, events and other activities.

All laundry is done in the home, residents helping as far as their capabilities will allow them. Because domestic tasks are done within the premises, the overall lifestyle of the residents becomes very domestic and non-institutional.

Site context

Flat, semi-rural site on the edges of a large town west of Helsinki.

Philosophy of care

To provide professional high-quality care in a suitable environment. With professional and skilled staff, a positive working environment and a stimulating day-to-day lifestyle, residents can live a humane life in a meaningful way.

The purpose and goals are:
* *To give residents a good quality of life: create individual care plans*
* *Maintain the sense of belonging to a community: provide adequate support and develop group activities and create comfortable living within the community*
* *Educated staff: training and up to date information*
* *Premises are up to date and in accordance with their intended uses*
* *Finances are stable enough so as not to endanger basic operations*

Philosophy expression in the building design

The factors that describe the communal nature of this home are:
* *The community becomes a family, residents live as a big family*
* *Home-like surroundings, residents can bring their own furniture*
* *Safety and serenity*

Kitchen can be used for all cooking activities using the central island. Glass cabinets allow residents to see contents, and not rummage through other cupboards. Gate and flap can make kitchen private if necessary.

Lounge: Paintings, tissue paper stained glass and curtains have all been made by residents as activities. Upper floor has staff facilities – the open tread staircase is to discourage residents from using this stair as well as allowing view through. Nevertheless there is a gate at the bottom of the stair which is tied shut. Daylight and well-proportioned room give a feeling of spaciousness.

Residents' own furniture, in a mixture of styles give a feeling of domesticity; in most peoples homes furniture is acquired over a period of time, not all at once. **There is little contrast between walls, floors and door handles.** The interior finishes are a backdrop to the paintings and furniture.

- *Closeness, togetherness*
- *Good access to external spaces*
- *Trained and skilled staff always nearby*
- *Suitable medical treatment is available*
- *Stimulating environment: different spaces, windows and daylight*
- *Creative action and interaction*
- *Staff and residents live a normal life together e.g. cooking food together*
- *Supporting physical and human resource"*

Aspects of the building design that work well and which are worth repeating
Small, cosy bedrooms support residents' safety and security and also encourage residents to spend more time in the common areas, with other residents.

Other comments
Lack of contrast between floors, walls, doors and door handles can be problematic for people with impaired vision.

AUTHOR'S COMMENT
Opri Ja Oleski is a very interesting building in that the building serves as a backdrop for the activities that take place, and it enables diverse and stimulating activities to take place. Overall this is one large family living together.

The philosophy of care was carefully thought out and planned first by the owner. The design of the building then followed on from this. The open plan nature of the common areas allows for a homely atmosphere when everyone can see what is happening.

Mornings are used as a peaceful quiet time for individuals. Afternoons are 'family' activities. Residents all have a say in planning activities and are recorded in a daily activity book. These include:
- Visiting art teacher on a weekly basis. Students from the local art college have participated in activities with the residents
- One major art project every year
- Visiting physiotherapist bi-weekly
- Visiting actors – stimulating memories and emotions. There is funding for a future theatre project
- Singing and dancing
- Literature discussions
- Themes to bedroom corridors, e.g. birds – with pictures, charts and sounds of birds
- Garden areas are used as a living room in the summer, clearing snow is a winter activity
- Garden planting has rhymes and poems on small tags which can be read by residents and staff. Residents selected the verses and made these tags
- Fence panel decorated as a farmhouse wall is familiar for many of the residents brought up in the countryside.

Bedroom corridor: Changing themes in corridor - birds is the current theme with pictures, wallchart, and piped sounds of birdsong. **White door handles are difficult to see against a white door. Coloured architraves and skirting boards frame doors and wall/floor junctions but greater contrast would be preferred. An improvised note to tell residents that a wc is behind this door is disappointing.**

Thus there are residents' paintings on the wall, homemade curtains, tissue paper stained glass on the windows, etc. bringing a sense of life to the home and identification as residents can recognise the curtains or paintings that they have made. Taller bright spaces in the lounge, lowered ceilings in dining and kitchen areas, quieter and darker corridor areas by the bedrooms are all carefully proportioned spaces.

Residents' own furniture and the mixture of furniture styles contribute to a domestic appearance to the interiors (in most peoples' homes furniture is acquired over a period of time, not all at once). In Scandinavia the winter days can be very short, and getting the most out of daylight is essential.

There is the danger that the spaces could feel more like a school classroom or art gallery, but the spatial design, proportion and use of daylight has cleverly avoided this and a domestic scale pervades.

Bedroom sizes are the smallest practical, the intention from the outset being to maximise space for the communal areas and to encourage residents to participate in group activities. They claim that people with dementia also feel more secure in a smaller space such as these bedrooms. This is interesting when compared with bedroom sizes in Sweden, which are virtually studio apartments. A low level window allows views outside from the bed.

Only four of the bedrooms have an en-suite and that is a wc and washbasin only. Many of the residents are unable to use the wc unaided and to provide an en-suite to them is perceived as a risk. The concept of a sauna and shower as a daily routine is very common in Finland, and residents here will have been used to a lifestyle that involves this. Again this is part of the daily routine of the 'family' and there is a changing area, shower and sauna facility which is used everyday.

Staff facilities are located in a central first floor area. The open tread stair allows views through and also discourages residents from trying to climb up the stairs. Nevertheless there is a gate tied shut at the bottom of the stairs.

The garden area has been carefully thought out and is an ongoing project. The poetry tags on the trees and planting are a novel and innovative form of stimulation; some residents happily spend all afternoon reading the verses from the tags. A fence panel resembling a farmhouse wall, painted traditional Scandinavian red, with a mock window and curtains, and cut-out chickens creates a typical rural Finnish scene. Another fence panel is currently being painted as a country landscape and there will be cut-out cows. When viewed from inside the appearance will be of rural scenes, not of a fence. A small bridge will be built over a flower bed, similar to a bridge over a stream. The covered terrace area is well-used as another common space in the summer months.

Externally the building looks like any other house in the neighbourhood. Stained and painted timber cladding, timber doors and windows, brickwork and pitched roof are all familiar domestic materials and finishes. Therefore the building does not stand out as being any different from the other houses in the neighbourhood.

Overall, the success of Opra ja Oleski is based in a carefully thought-out concept of care and the building provides the space and the backdrop to allow this to take place.

➤ **The internal finishes are of painted timber floorboards, painted walls, doors, ceilings and joinery, all in neutral colours so as not to distract from the residents' artwork. However, whilst architraves and skirting boards do contrast with floor and wall, all doors are the same regardless of the function behind and the same colour as the surrounding wall and white door handles are nearly invisible against the white door.**

Fence panel decorated to look like a farmhouse wall: Including cut-out chickens, and external light fitting. Many residents have grown up in the countryside and these would be a familiar images. Tags on tree are verses and rhymes written and tied to trees as an activity. Residents in the garden can read these and reminisce.

The Peele

REASONS FOR SELECTION
➤ **Urban backland site**
➤ **Multi-storey building**
➤ **Open-plan common areas**
➤ **Each household on each floor has a different layout**

THE PEELE
Walney Road
Wythenshawe
Manchester
M22 9TG
Great Britain

Contact for further information
Huw John, Chief Executive Officer
huw.john@manchestercare.org.uk

Owner Manchester Care

Website www.manchestercare.org.uk

Entrance courtyard and garden: Overall appearance is of an apartment block or hotel, not a care home. Porch identifies main entrance gate for visitors. Garden area is accessed from either the end of the ground floor or from the entrance courtyard. Details as the other garden photograph. Brick wall and railings are for security to outside but still allow views out, and in. Multi-purpose room is on the first floor above the entrance. There is also a communal sitting area by the front door which is also popular for residents to watch the daily activity.

Open Since
January 2006

Architect
Pozzoni Design Group, Altrincham

Resident profile
Initially the home will be registered for 108 residential care, but this will soon become 96 residential care and 12 intermediate (nursing) care.
Following this, at least one ground floor household will be for residents with dementia but this is awaiting resolution of dementia registration criteria with the local authority.

1. Bedroom	9. Staff Base
2. Ensuite	10. Store
3. Lounge	11. Entrance
4. Activity	12. Office
5. Dining	13. Staff Changing
6. Kitchenette	14. Kitchen
7. WC	15. Meeeting/interview
8. Assisted Bath	16. Sluice

Number of residents
Three households of 11 residents
Three households of 12 residents
Three households of 13 residents
108 residents total

Typical bedroom floor area
14sq.m plus 4sq.m en-suite; 18sq.m

Floor area of each household
370sq.m for the 11 resident household
408sq.m for the 12 resident household
415sq.m for the 13 resident household

Building density
33sq.m /resident

Site area
6420sq.m

Site density
59sq.m /resident

Staffing
For the 96 residential care residents the staff are:

Morning:	One manager and one support manager
	Three care officers
	12 care assistants
	One cook
	Two catering assistants
	Two activity co-ordinators
	Six housekeeping assistants
	Two laundry assistants

All households have access to an external space. Large windows maximise natural daylight into bedrooms and the small windows allow for views outside from beds. Black tarmacadam provides a continuous surface and the contrasting granite setts clearly define the pathway edge.

Open Plan communal area: Bedroom door can be seen from this area as can the dining area and kitchen opening, helping those with impaired memory to see their way around. Fire regulations required an opening with fire shutter to the kitchen and not totally open-plan as originally envisaged. Change of floor colour by balcony door is of a similar tone to avoid appearance of a step.

Bedroom doors: Recess from circulation area, lower ceiling and downlighter create a 'porch' type of space. Memory boxes are for residents' personal items which help residents identify their own door. The return wall is a different colour to define corners clearly and handrail contrasting with the wall and wall/floor colour contrasts. This all helps people with impaired vision.

Dining area: Runners on chairs prevent tipping over. Variety in lighting and ceiling heights help define spaces. Flooring has a matt finish to reduce glare.

Afternoon: As above but nine care assistants
Evening: One manager and one support manager
                Three care officers
                Nine care assistants
Night: Three care officers
                Seven care assistants

For the 12 intermediate(nursing) care residents the staff will be:
One team leader; seven staff nurses; three assistant practitioners.

These staffing levels will be reviewed when the registration criteria for dementia have been resolved. Building and landscape maintenance will be provided by contract staff.

Service and ancillary space
Each household has a small kitchenette, assisted bathroom, staff base and storage. There is a central kitchen, laundry, staff facilities, offices and administration.

Meals and laundry
Breakfast and snacks are prepared within each household by housekeeping staff. Lunch and dinner are prepared in the main kitchen and brought to each household via a hot trolley and then served to residents in the dining area of each household. The hot trolley allows meals to be kept warm so residents do not have to be interrupted if they are participating in an activity. There are, however, regulations dictating the maximum length of time that food can be kept in such an arrangement.

At the time of writing all the residents have moved to The Peele from other care homes, where there were set meal times. With residents being accustomed to having set meal times the management have decided not to change this routine in the light of the upheaval of moving to a new home. It is envisaged that as residents, their families and staff settle in to their new home then new routines for meals will evolve.

All clothes and linen is done in the central laundry.

Site context
Flat backland site located in a local authority housing estate.

Philosophy of care
Manchester Care mission statement and approach to all their properties is:
To offer a range of quality care services to people in their local communities by providing professional care and support from committed, skilled and properly trained staff.

Manchester Care homes are busy and friendly with a variety of opportunities for social activity and leisure pursuits. Whether residents are with us for a short stay, a planned programme of rehabilitation or for long term care, they can be sure of a warm welcome and a high standard of care and support.

Quality and excellence: The key to the service we provide is the quality of staff, who undergo specialised training so they can provide a high standard of assessment, care and support to residents. Staff work towards national qualifications in care and are dedicated to improving continuously the care they provide.

Manchester Care also employ activities organisers who co-ordinate a range of activities, hobbies, events and excursions and enable residents and relatives to have a say in the running of their home.

Amenities and facilities: Each home has its own dedicated catering team providing a choice of home-cooked meals. All specialised diets are catered for. The gardens around our homes provide areas for relaxation on warmer days as well as pleasant views all year round. Away from the bustle of the reception area, there are quieter lounges for peace and relaxation, communal living rooms with TV, radio and areas set aside for smokers.

Innovations in care: Manchester Care leads the way in developing new and better ways of providing effective care. Manchester Care continually updates care practices in relation to continence, diabetes, sensory impairment, dental and oral care. Manchester Care also promote health and safety programmes among staff to maximise service user support. Manchester Care takes seriously our duty to support frail and vulnerable older people and has pioneered sensitive protocols to protect residents.

All our residential care homes have their own management team who are responsible for the day-to-day running of the home. A full management and operational support service is provided by head office in relation to care practices, health and safety issues, finance, facilities management and catering operations.

Kitchen: Resident-accessible items are stored in cupboards with no doors so these items can be readily seen. The principle of the lowered worktop is to allow sitting or wheelchair access. Sink taps are traditional and familiar cross head taps and separate hot and cold.

Balcony detail: Whilst there are no residents with dementia on the upper floors, demographics may change in the future. The whole building is designed on dementia principles. To avoid climbing risks to the balcony the handrail height is 1.2metre and there is no foothold on the inside face. The height is also comfortable enough to lean on when standing. Perforated panels allow light in and views out but avoids any feeling of vertigo that might occur in some people if this were a clear or open panel.

Philosophy expression in the building design

Whilst this building is not exclusively for dementia care, the principles of dementia care have been applied throughout. This allows a resident to continue living in their room should their condition change and allows greater flexibility in future use. Nothing has to fundamentally change with the building should there be a greater, or smaller, requirement for residents with dementia in the future.

Each household is of a different layout to the others on that floor, creating individuality and allowing each household to develop its own character.

As far as possible, open plan areas with high ceilings and lots of daylight have been created. The corridors have been kept to a minimum length.

Aspects of the building design that work well and which are worth repeating

At the time of writing there is little evidence about use but staff have commented favourably on the open common lounge, dining, activity areas. The dual aspect to the 11 resident household has been particularly well received.

The backland site makes it difficult for everyday street activity in the neighbourhood to be observed by residents so by having the entrance courtyard garden area and the front door set back into the courtyard, this brings activity into the home.

Other comments

The open plan common areas on the upper floors of a care home presented challenges in terms of fire safety engineering. After much dialogue with the local fire officer an 'Aquamist' fire suppression system combined with a robust fire management strategy allowed the open plan concept to be realised.

The legislation requiring lobbies to fire escape stairs in multi-storey buildings could not be overcome and consequently corridors end in a door, not in a small alcove and window as originally envisaged.

The first generation of staff and residents have been transferred to The Peele from other nearby homes, which were 30-40 years old and obsolete. There has been a settling in period whilst staff and residents get used to the new open plan layouts.

AUTHOR'S COMMENT

Since I have worked on the design of this building I asked Stephen Judd, one of the authors of 'Design for Dementia' to visit The Peele and comment. Dr Judd is Chief Executive of The Hammond Care Group, Australia's leading dementia service provider. He writes:

"The Peele is, I understand, the first of a new generation of buildings for Manchester Care. The size of the households is influenced by the economics of staffing and also the wish to create domestic environments. 11-13 residents allows for small group living and efficient staffing.

Bedroom: Small window and low window cills maximise views out from bed or when sitting and bring more daylight in. Residents can bring their own furniture and ornaments.

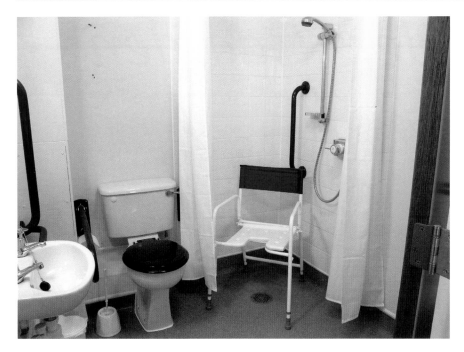

Ensuite: Grabrails, toilet seat, toilet roll holder, chair-back are easy to see with their contrast to the walls. The wc is traditional and familiar looking and can be seen from the bed; separate hot and cold crosshead taps are also familiar and recognisable.

The variety in household and room layouts along with different en-suite arrangements, bay windows, etc. does encourage greater individuality.

The open plan common areas were a fundamental design concept. There is good way-finding; there is no doubt that residents can see or sense where they are or where they want to go. Site constraints meant that there are corridors. I think the architect would have preferred to have none but my view is that they are fine and encourage separation between bedrooms and common areas. The orientation of the common areas allows for direct morning or afternoon sun.

Kitchenettes in each household are intended for breakfast, lunch, drinks and snacks only. It is unfortunate that, apparently, regulations required these to be separate rooms so a large opening has been created with a hidden fire shutter. It is pleasing that the opening allows the sounds and smells of food to stimulate residents in the lounge area. However, there is the unfortunate operational aspect that there are set meal times. I am advised that meals can be kept warm whilst residents finish an activity – I am not sure if this occurs in practice.

The door recess to each bedroom creates a semi-personal space. Lowered ceiling, downlight and memory box allow for this area to be personalised by individual residents. Some rooms have a large bay window and a smaller lower window, allowing a resident to look outside when in bed. Some of the bedrooms without bay windows have an en-suite with an external window. North facing bedrooms do not get direct sunlight but do have a view over the adjoining school playground and its activity and I certainly found the outlook of these rooms quite charming.

Differing heights to the ceilings help to define spaces. Access for plant and equipment services is required but areas of non-domestic lay-in grid ceiling tiles are kept to a minimum.

Each household has either its own garden, or a large balcony with a view over the garden areas or the entrance courtyard. There is a secure garden area to the south-east corner of the site by the entrance from the road. Six of the households have views into the entrance courtyard allowing residents to watch daily life taking place so they can still feel part of the world at large. I still would like residents to have access to the outside – not simply look out on it. It will be interesting to see if staff practices actually take residents outside.

I visited the Peele soon after it was opened and in my view the biggest challenge will be that its staffing and its residents have come from four separate environments and been 'melded' together. That is a huge cultural challenge. The environment that has been created on an awkward site will go far to facilitate this – but I look forward to revisiting this service in five years' to see if it the staff and management have made it happen."

Garden: The walking path loops back to the start and granite setts clearly define the edge. Picket fence is a familiar detail to many people and separates sitting area from walking area. This is to reduce the perceived size and scale of a large garden; most residents have lived in back-to-back terraced housing all their lives with a small back yard and are more familiar with smaller outdoor spaces. This photograph was taken before completion; seating, further planting and lockable gate on tall fence are yet to be installed.

Ros-Anders Gaarden

ROS-ANDERS GAARDEN
Rosvaegan 5
S-13756
Tungelsta
Sweden

Contact for further information
Rolf Ljungstrom Rolf.ljungstrom@haninge.se

Owner Haninge Elderly Care Administration

Website www.haninge.se

External appearance is similar to other domestic buildings in the neighbourhood. Entrance is on the corner. French balconies are the corner doors.

Open since
May 1999

Architect
ANOVA arkiteckter AB, Stockholm

Resident profile
All residents have dementia. Originally there was a mix of residents with dementia and residents with physical disabilities.

Number of residents
Four households of ten residents; 40 resident total

Typical bedroom floor area
24.76sq.m and 25.23sq.m plus 5.7sq.m ensuite: 30.46sq.m and 30.93sq.m total

Floor area of each household
561.7sq.m

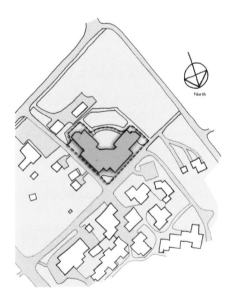

North

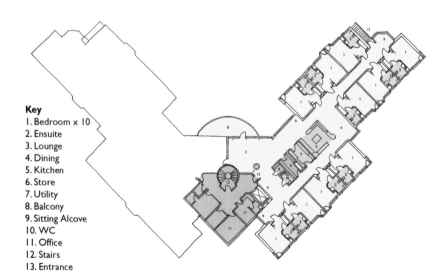

Key
1. Bedroom x 10
2. Ensuite
3. Lounge
4. Dining
5. Kitchen
6. Store
7. Utility
8. Balcony
9. Sitting Alcove
10. WC
11. Office
12. Stairs
13. Entrance

Building density
56sq.m per resident

Site area
4662sq.m

Site density
116.5sq.m per resident

Staffing
Five management and administration staff.
38 care staff for the whole building and all staff have multi-tasking roles, with the exception of the nurse. The building is also used as the base for local home health operations.

Service and ancillary space
Each household has its own kitchen, laundry and storage.
Office and administration space is located between the two households on each floor and on the third floor only.
The kitchen also serves as the staff base for each household.

Meals and laundry
Each household is self-contained and operates independently from the others in the building. The kitchen is the centre of each household and all meals are prepared entirely here by the staff, with residents helping as far as they are able to do so in setting the table, etc. Menus are determined in full discussion with the residents. With three meals a day, the preparation, eating and cleaning up becomes the focus for the day for most residents.
Laundry is also undertaken within each household.

Site context
Flat suburban site on a quiet road in a small commuter town south of Stockholm.

Philosophy of care
To give good health care in a home environment and to create a meaningful life for the residents. Great respect and consideration is given to the individual's needs and wishes.

Swedish legislation requires that the interior of a care home should have the qualities of a private home in the design, and the layout to be easily understood from any point in the building. The motto for any design should be, from an elderly person's point of view easy to see, to orientate in, and express values which are found in the decorating of private homes and domestic

Alcove at end of corridor creates an 'event', not a dead end. This is a quiet area as an alternative space to the more active lounge and dining areas.

Lounge: The fireplace is little used and is used more by residents as a wayfinding object. The connecting door to the adjacent household is shown open but is usually closed and is for staff use only. Front door to household is fully glazed which can present problems with residents wanting to 'explore'. Table in foreground is for activities, there is a separate dining area. Overall impression is of a homely domesticity but the **suspended ceiling detracts from this.**

Kitchen and dining: Open plan allows kitchen sounds and smells to stimulate residents through the household acting as stimulation for mealtimes. Lowered worktops allow for resident involvement and gate can make kitchen area secure if necessary. Gate also folds back against wall so as to be unobtrusive. Walking route from lounge goes around the kitchen and dining room and along bedroom corridor. See bedroom door/corridor photograph regarding floor finish.

Bedroom: Size is more of a studio apartment with sufficient space for a sitting area and sleeping area. There is a small kitchenette which allows residents to make their own drinks/snacks, not having to go to the kitchen and thus reinforcing a sense of independence. Services can be disconnected if required. Every room has either a bay window or corner window to maximise daylight and alternative views out.

architecture. The design should avoid an institutional-like appearance. Ros-Anders Gaarden is homelike due to its colour (wallpapers) on the walls, and the timber floor, common in many Scandinavian houses.

Philosophy expression in the building design
- *Households of ten residents allows for small group living. The layout of the households allows residents to gather together and participate in activities or to be alone in quiet alcoves*
- *Room sizes are large enough to be like studio apartments rather than bedrooms and have generous storage and a small kitchenette*
- *The kitchen is the focus for each household*
- *The residents participate in the planning of their own care, health care and service so personal dignity and a sense of control over their own lives is maintained*
- *The architects have stated that the design in the commonly shared parts of each household is intended "as an urban milieu or whole environment, where the openness between different functions in the room could be interpreted as an standing invitation to participate or not – a room without mental thresholds.*

Aspects of the building design that work well and which are worth repeating
- *Central kitchen acts as a focus for each household*
- *The layout of the household creates an internal route for walking around via different spaces. This is important in the winter when the weather may be too severe to go outside.*
- *Finishes and colours on floors and walls are typical of domestic Scandinavian interiors.*

Other comments
- *Staff rooms are small.*
- *Dark squares inset into the flooring are perceived by some residents as holes*
- *The fireplace in the lounge is little used because the absence of a guarding could present a risk of residents harming themselves or putting objects into the fire*
- *There is no separate meeting room, lounge or multi-purpose room for families or for other meetings such as gatherings for all residents and staff (e.g. Christmas parties)*
- *The staff base in the kitchen is not popular with the staff and they would prefer a separate room as a base. This is for the practical reasons of not risking paperwork getting soiled with kitchen mess, as well as not being able to leave files unattended if called away*
- *Access to the ground floor garden is through either of the ground floor households. Therefore residents to the first floor must pass through another household to reach the garden and this is not a preferred situation at all.*

AUTHOR'S COMMENT
Ros-Anders Gaarden has the look and feel of a Swedish home, especially with the use of timber floor finishes throughout. The use of polished timber floors is a cultural issue. People who have spent their lives in Scandinavia and are used to seeing glare and reflections on polished timber floors are therefore familiar with this appearance.

In other countries this is not a familiar ◄ appearance and the floor could be perceived as having a wet appearance, which would deter people from walking on this floor.

The kitchen is very large and is the focus for each household. Residents are drawn to this area as most activity occurs here. Staff working here can also see most of the household and residents can engage with the staff in the kitchen at different points, both on the dining side and within the kitchen area itself.

To relieve the appearance of the floors there ◄ are panels of dark blue squares. To someone with dementia this could be perceived as a 'hole' and some people would walk around this as a consequence.

Having each household operate independently as its own self-contained unit, with the staff multitasking, is the key to the domesticity of each household. In your own home everyone undertakes several chores, and by not having different staff (e.g. cleaners, cooks) coming into the house, a degree of daily routine and familiarity can be established.

Resident involvement is also crucial. For each resident, life in each household becomes a continuation of their own lives before they came to live here, with daily routines and tasks undertaken, as you would in your own home. This is undertaken as far as possible considering each resident's capabilities.

The internal walking route accommodates the long, cold winter nights in Sweden. The route has events on the way, such as seating alcoves, corner windows, quiet sitting areas which makes the route a series of events, not just a racetrack circuit. Seating alcoves with large windows at the end of each corridor also provide quiet areas and view to the outside as well as daylight to the interior. In Scandinavia the winter days can be very short, and getting the most out of daylight is essential.

The furniture generally has a domestic look to it, and small touches such as vases of flowers and potted plants help with this. The fireplace in the living room area is also typically Swedish.

Bedroom ceilings are a conventional plasterboard finish. The bedrooms are very generously sized and are more like studio apartments than bedrooms. The doors have been designed to look like the front door to an apartment with a frosted glass sidelight to allow borrowed daylight into the corridor. The hallway to each room is large enough for built-in storage cupboards, a hat/coat stand and a vertical slatted dividing screen offers privacy to the sleeping area from the door without obscuring vision.

The main area of the bedroom is large enough for a sleeping area and lounge area with tv, settee and table. Each room has either a corner window or a bay window and all have a French balcony i.e. door that opens inwards with a handrail and guarding across the opening. All the rooms on the first floor also have a small kitchenette for making tea or coffee, which is very useful for visits, which can be from neighbours within the household as well as families. Providing this ensures that the residents can still maintain a degree of independence, by not having to go to the kitchen for a drink or snack.

The en-suites are all on external walls allowing for natural daylight in these rooms. There is an access hatch from within the en-suite to one of the built-in cupboards in the hall, allowing a resident (or staff) to get a fresh towel without leaving the en-suite.

Externally the building appears like the other houses in the neighbourhood. Walls are painted timber planks fixed to a concrete panel wall construction and the roof is steeply pitched with conventional roof tiles. The design of the building has been adapted to the building plan for the town of Tungelsta, which stipulates the placement of the building to one edge of the site in order to promote the concept of a garden to each building. The building height is restricted to two floors.

The name of the care home comes from a former gardener that used the premises. The gardener was in particular famous for his roses and was known as Ros-Anders. Tungelsta as a town is known for its flowers and vegetables. Ros-Anders Gaarden has a very comfortable, relaxed and domestic atmosphere and the building design goes a long way to enabling the concept of each household living as a family to be realised and creating a quality of domestic life.

Ensuite: Toilet cannot be seen from the bed and flooring turned up as a skirting board may be perceived as a continuation of the floor. There is no contrast between sanitaryware and wall tiling. The band of coloured tiles lowers the apparent height of the space

➤ **The suspended ceiling tiles throughout the communal areas do not give a domestic quality and detract from the otherwise homely atmosphere.**

Bedroom corridor: Reflections on a polished floor give the impression of water on the floor. Dark blue squares could also be perceived as 'holes' in the floor and some people would walk around them. Obscured glass sidelight allows some borrowed daylight into the corridor and outward opening door can be fully opened against wall if necessary. **Apart from a small nameplate there is nothing for a resident to identify their own door from another.**

Rosewood at Laurel Lake

REASONS FOR SELECTION

➤ **Independent cottage-like building**
➤ **'Eden Principles' of domestic, homelike environment and care applied***
➤ **Part of a large retirement community**
➤ **Building sits well in the site context**

*see www.edenalt.com for further information

ROSEWOOD at LAUREL LAKE
200 Laurel Lake Drive
Hudson
Ohio 44236
USA

Contact for further information
Kathy Bermeister, Tel: 1-3300-655-1406
Jim Herman, HGF Architects jherman@hgfarchitects.com

Owner Laurel Lake and Catholic Health Care Partners

Website www.laurellake.com

External appearance is of a typical suburban house. The garage doors are false, the kitchen is behind them.

Open since
August 2004

Architect
Herman Gibans Fodor Inc., Cleveland, Ohio

Resident profile
14 residents with dementia live at Rosewood. Rosewood is part of a large continuing care retirement community consisting of 300 independent living units, 53 assisted living and 75 skilled nursing care.

No of residents
14 residents
Six single rooms plus four double rooms

Typical bedroom floor area
13.0sq.m plus 5.1sq.m ensuite for double rooms;
18.1sq.m for single rooms

Floor area of household
708.8sq.m

Building density
50sq.m per resident

Key
1. Bedroom
2. Ensuite
3. Living Room
4. Dining
5. Kitchen
6. Restricted Kitchen
7. Store
8. Sunroom
9. Garden
10. Utility Room
11. Sluice
12. Plant room
13. Bath
14. WC
15. Medicine Store
16. Entrance Hall
17. Connecting corridor
18. Staff Base

Site area

150acres for the whole Laurel Lakes community (607,035sq.m)

Staffing

1 to 7 staff ratio

6:30am – 3:00pm   two nursing assistants with one nurse from 8:30am – 4:00pm

2:30pm - 8:00pm   two nursing assistants

Overnight   one nursing assistant

Nursing assistants undertake duties with food preparation, laundry, activities.

Service and ancillary space

There is a food storage pantry behind the kitchen which stores enough for two to three days ahead. The principal kitchen is hidden so only domestic-looking cupboards and appliances are visible. Staff desk is located in the kitchen with a hatch in the wall for views into the lounge area and over the worktop into the dining area.

Meals and laundry

Meals are prepared in the house. There is a 'visible' kitchenette where residents can be involved in food preparation as far as their capabilities and regulations will allow them. Behind the kitchenette is the household kitchen which contains the cooker, dishwasher, etc. Ingredients are brought here from the main central kitchen to the whole development every three days.

The breakfast bar arrangement allows residents to sit and still be involved with kitchen activities if they cannot access the kitchen space itself. Residents also help with serving and washing up. There is flexibility in meals and meal times because of the independence from the main kitchen.

There is a utility room in Rosewood in addition to the main laundry for the whole development.

Site context

Rosewood is a cottage in part of a large continuing care retirement community of 450 residents set in 150acres of landscaped grounds. The adjoining buildings are three storey retirement apartments and single storey retirement villas. The community is located in a suburb of Hudson, Ohio.

Philosophy of care

Laurel Lake's aim is to enhance and enrich the quality of life for older adults by encouraging wellness, self-determination and independence through life's transitions. Laurel Lake is committed to providing a lifestyle that brings dignity to all residents. While there's no place like home, we are committed to providing our residents' personal care.

Dining area with lounge through door, kitchen on the right. This is a bright and airy room with access to the garden, compared to the windowless lounge. Carpet on the floor which is unusual in a dining area. Fire door is recessed and decorated to look like part of the wall.

Kitchen: Domestic-looking kitchen units are in the areas that can be seen, non-domestic catering-style kitchen equipment is in the hidden kitchen. Island worktop allows for facing the dining room when working in the kitchen. The lower worktop allows residents to sit and become involved with kitchen activity. The staff base is part of the kitchen fittings and there is an opening into the lounge. There is no door between the kitchen and dining room; residents are free to walk into the kitchen.

Philosophy expression in the building design
Rosewood is designed as a small-scale residential setting that provides residents and staff with a home-like environment. The small household permits residents to live as close as possible to normal life and creates an environment where staff can provide truly person-centered care.

The heart of Rosewood is a family-sized kitchen area which allows variable snacking and dining as well as residents' participation in meal preparation, serving and washing up.

The residents' living room has indirect cove lighting, a built-in entertainment centre and display shelving. The dining area has ample daylight and the dining area and sun-room both open out to a secure courtyard garden area. Handrails are disguised as dado rails.

Whilst Rosewood is larger than the neighbouring retirement villas, the form, scale and detailing allows Rosewood to blend in with the neighbouring properties. There are even false garage doors to match the adjoining villas.

Each bedroom has a memory box outside the front door and residents are encouraged to bring their own furniture. Display shelves allow for personal decoration. En-suite rooms have a shower, wc and washbasin and contrasting tiling helps with visual cueing.

Aspects of the building design that work well and which are worth repeating
The kitchen layout of a low worktop and appliances and worktops facing outwards allows resident involvement in the kitchen activity and also acts as a focus for the household. The hidden kitchen avoids any institutional appearance from catering-style fittings and also allows any potentially hazardous activities to be carried out safely.

Access to courtyard garden from dining room and sunroom. Garden layout also allows for secure views of outside world over a fence and trellis.

Service access to the main building through a 'hidden' door. A separate front door to the outside reinforces domesticity, independence and is convenient for family visits.

Other comments
• *Looped bedroom corridor, whilst creating a walking route, does not have enough variety or points of interest.*
• *No external views or daylight to the living room make this a very inward looking space which is dominated by the television.*

AUTHOR'S COMMENTS
Rosewood successfully takes on board the 'Eden principles'* (www.edenalt.com) which aim to create a domestic homelike environment and provide care to match. The scale and form is that of a large single storey house.

Hidden door for staff-only access to the rest of the Laurel Lakes development.

The living room has no external windows and therefore no natural daylight, however the focus of this room is a large TV and entertainment centre built into the wall, so this is an inward looking room. Having some of the bedrooms accessed directly off of this space gets away from any dead end corridors situations and allows residents to feel more involved with the daily activity of the household. There are no reports of residents being disturbed from noise from the living room. The uplighters provide even glare-free lighting whilst spotlights pick out features, which all gives variety in lighting.

The other side of the building has bedrooms accessed from a looping corridor, which creates a walking route but not in the same 'series of events' way as the Scandinavian homes do. This looping corridor creates a central space where the service rooms are located. This maximizes external walls for bedrooms.

Having two distinct halves to the building also helps orientation; residents can recognise if their room is from the corridor side or the lounge side.

The central kitchen is a focus for the whole building. The Eden philosophy goes beyond just providing a domestic-looking kitchen but also to allow resident involvement in kitchen activities and this appears to be successful here. The position of the central worktop allows staff to face the residents if they are working in the kitchen and the lower breakfast bar allows residents to still be involved in the kitchen, even if they cannot come inside the kitchen itself. The dining area is bright and spacious and carpet is used on the floor, rather than vinyl, which softens the whole area. Fire doors between lounge and dining fold back against the wall and are painted out to blend in with the wall surround.

The sunroom is really just a covered veranda and is more like a separate room, rather than a continuation of the other common spaces. There is a hidden door which is access to an enclosed walkway to the main building and also access to the garden.

The courtyard garden is of a domestic scale, in which the paving allows a resident to wander in a loop between sunroom and dining room. Fencing is high enough not to be climbed but trellising to the top reduces the apparent height and neighbouring buildings can be seen. There is an external gate but this is the same design as the fence and is surrounded by soft landscaping, therefore it is not obviously a gate.

The atmosphere of Rosewood is of its own household and not part of a large development. There is the risk of separating the residents with dementia from the rest of the community but views out from bedrooms and gardens and the scale and appearance integrate Rosewood with its surrounding neighbourhood.

Bedroom doors: memory boxes are built into the walls with their own lighting. Name plates also have residents' photograph. The handrail looks like a dado rail and part of the wall panelling, not an institutional handrail as such.

Garden: Trellis fencing allows views out but is high enough to deter climbing.

Rosewood Court (Leeds)

REASONS FOR SELECTION

➤ **Self-contained 'extra care'* one-bedroom apartments for people with dementia**

➤ **Part of a larger development**

➤ **Multi-storey building**

➤ **Urban location**

* See 'philosophy of care' section

ROSEWOOD COURT
Moor Allerton Care Centre
4 Cranmer Close
Leeds LS17 5PU
Great Britain

Contact for further information
Sarah Fox, Care Centre Manager sarah.fox@mha.org.uk
or scheme.moorallerton@mha.org.uk

Owner MHA Care Group

Website www.mha.org.uk

Entrance: Rosewood Court is on ground and 1st floors, Yewtree Court extends over the second floor of the building.

Open since
November 2004

Architect
West and Machell, Leeds

Tenant profile
20 tenants with early stages of dementia.
There are also 45 elderly tenants and 5 intermediate care flats (Yew Tree Court) and a dementia day care service (Bay Tree Resource Centre) on the site.

Number of tenants
20 one-bedroom extra-care apartments for tenants living with dementia.
Yew Tree Court has 50 one and two bedroom extra care apartments.
Rosewood Court is two-storey, Yew Tree Court is three storey, part of the third storey is above Rosewood Court.

Typical floor areas of apartments
One bedroom apartments are 47sq.m, 51sq.m and 57sq.m (corner apartment)

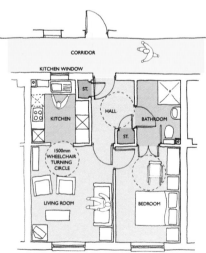

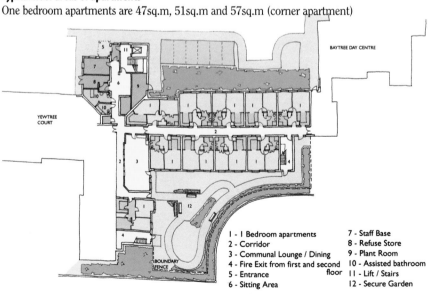

1 - 1 Bedroom apartments
2 - Corridor
3 - Communal Lounge / Dining
4 - Fire Exit from first and second floor
5 - Entrance
6 - Sitting Area
7 - Staff Base
8 - Refuse Store
9 - Plant Room
10 - Assisted bathroom
11 - Lift / Stairs
12 - Secure Garden

Building density (for Rosewood Court)
80sq.m per resident

Site area (for Rosewood Court)
1300sq.m

Site density
65sq.m/tenant

Staffing
Through out the whole development there are approximately 25 care staff, four management staff plus maintenance, kitchen staff, cleaning staff, etc. There are care staff on site for 24 hours every day.

Service and ancillary space
To Rosewood there is a communal lounge/dining to ground and first floor with a small kitchenette. There are two assisted bathrooms for Rosewood Court, all apartments have a shower.

Meals and laundry
All apartments have a kitchen with full cooking facilities. There is also a space and plumbing for a washing machine if a tenant would want to install their own but there is not the space or vents for a tumble dryer.

Tenants also have the option of having meals prepared in the kitchen (attached to the café of Yewtree Court) and having them brought to either their apartment or the communal dining/lounge on the ground or first floor or eating in the cafe.

The café to Yew Tree Court can be used by Rosewood Court tenants. However access is either via locked doors (requiring staff to open) or by leaving Rosewood Court and entering Yew Tree Court via their main entrance.

Kitchen in apartment with window to corridor and personal ornaments placed on cill. Separate oven and hob could be difficult for some people as a separate cooker with oven, hob and grill is more common to the UK. Cooking hob contrasts well with worktop but fleck effect on the worktop could be perceived as crumbs. Space where pedal bin is seen here is for a washing machine. Right hand cupboard contains cut-off switches and can be locked if a resident is likely accidentally to turn the services off or if services need to be disconnected for the resident's safety.

Corridor to apartments: The kitchen window on the left is popular with residents for social contact. Front doors are different colours and a small recessed shelf is for personalising the front door. However, residents seem to prefer to place personal objects in the window and not the shelf area. Doorbell surround contrasts with wall to help make its location obvious. Handrails contrast well with wall and the subtle change of wall colour may not be noticed by some residents but it does help to break up the otherwise large expanse of wall. Low ceiling and minimum width create a tight feeling to the corridor.

There is a communal laundry to Yew Tree Court which Rosewood Court tenants can use (access as above) or with staff assistance. There is an outside clothes drying areas accessed from the laundry.

Site context
A leveled off site in the middle of a local authority housing estate, close to local shops.

Philosophy of care
MHA mission and values statement is:

We are a charity striving to combine professional standards, top class management and financial sustainability in providing older people with a caring service based on Christian principles. Our values underpin all our work which may be summarized as:
- *High quality, person centred care and support for older people*
- *Founded on compassion and respect for individuals' dignity and personal choice*
- *Focused on nuturing a person's spiritual and physical well-being.*

Regarding Extra Care*, MHA define this as:
To provide personal, domestic, social and emotional care with a rehabilitative focus to enable service users to continue to live in their own home and maintain as far as possible their independence and usual lifestyle.

Extra Care offers an alternative to residential care for frail older people which combines the advantages of high quality, self contained accommodation and the provision of flexible care services based in the centre. The service enables service users to retain control over their own lives while receiving the support they need in a secure environment.

Philosophy expression in the building design
Rosewood Court provides independent living in apartments with the opportunity for social contact in the communal spaces.

MHA have strived to achieve a home from home feel that is safe by having well lit areas with good signage, use of colors to prompt orientation, recognisable fixtures and fittings, and safe garden areas with walking paths.

Communal areas and entrances have fully integrated door entry and security systems and isolation switches are in lockable cupboards to prevent accidental turning off or unsafe usage. Assistive technology is also used and is constantly reviewed to address the changing needs of tenants.

Are there any aspects of the building design that work well and are worth repeating?
The café to Yew Tree Court is a success and is used by the tenants of Rosewood Court.

Access to the bathroom in each apartment from either the hallway or bedroom works well. Full height floor-ceiling doors allow for the installation of a ceiling hoist from bedroom to en-suite, if required.

South facing garden area has sunlight all day.

The window from the kitchen into the corridor is very popular with tenants of Rosewood Court. Tenants have reported that they feel more secure when they can see there are other people in the building and they can check on their neighbours. Most tenants of Yew Tree Court, however, have fitted curtains or blinds to their kitchen/corridor windows for more privacy.

Other comments

Corridors appear long and narrow with little natural daylight. The apartment front doors at Yew Tree Court are recessed from the corridor creating a 'porch' type of space. Rosewood Court front doors do not have this same large recess. There is a small recessed shelf by the front door for milk delivery. These shelves are often used for placing personal objects, flowers, etc.

There is no ventilation to the corridor areas and these spaces can get very warm in the summer.

Sitting area to the entrance of Rosewood Court is little used as there are no direct views outside. All tenants prefer to use the communal lounge/dining room on the ground floor. The first floor communal lounge is used for social events, tenant meetings or certain activities.

AUTHOR'S COMMENTS

Rosewood Court differs from other places in this publication as it provides a self-contained apartment for people with dementia. At the time of writing all flats are single occupancy but there is the opportunity for couples to live here, should one of the partners have dementia. The alternative is either increased stress for one partner trying to cope in a non-dementia friendly environment or for the couple to effectively live apart, with one partner in a residential home.

Rosewood Court is for people with the early stages of dementia. Staff make every effort to adapt care to meet changing needs and increase care input as dementia advances in order that a tenant can remain in their flat for as long as possible. Should an individual find it more difficult to cope in this environment they would be relocated to a more suitable home.

The layout of the one-bedroom apartments themselves is the same for both Rosewood Court and Yew Tree Court, the dementia design aspects applying to both units. The difference between the two is chiefly that Yew Tree Court has more communal facilities such as the café, laundry, and hairdresser. Rosewood Court tenants have to be accompanied by staff though locked doors if they wish to use these facilities. All the apartments are of the same layout, except for the corners which are of a different layout.

Communal lounge on the ground floor with dining tables and kitchen area behind, located in an internal corner of the building, which reduces the opportunity for natural daylight and views out. This is mitigated by having the inward-looking activities of dining and kitchen to the rear and the sitting areas by the windows. Different lighting allows for variations in lighting control.

Garden area faces south to have direct sunlight all day. Raised planting beds and bird-table provide activity for residents. Change in surface materials could be an issue but no problems have been reported. All paths lead back into the building. **The door from the communal lounge is in the corner and because of proximity to bedroom windows, there cannot be an outdoor sitting area immediately by the communal lounge.**

The layout of each apartment is no different to any one-bedroom apartment. The entrance hall is large enough for storing wheelchairs or walking aids and there are two built in storage cupboards. There is a door to the bathroom from the hallway, as there would be in any apartment, so a tenant does not have to go via their bedroom if it were an en-suite only arrangement.

The living room to each apartment has a low window cill allowing views out when sitting, either to the garden area or the activity of the shops on the other side of the road. The living rooms to Yew Tree Court have a French balcony, i.e. double doors that open inwards and a handrail and guarding across the opening, but Rosewood Court does not have this. There is a danger of people with dementia wanting to climb over barriers, hence conventional windows (with restrictor stays to limit their opening width) to Rosewood Court.

There are sensors to the apartment front doors which can alert staff should a resident leave their apartment, at night, or at any other unusual time. These are only turned on based on a specific risk assessment. Others sensors could be added if risks warranted this.

The bedrooms also have a low cill allowing views out from the bed. There is a full floor to ceiling high double door from the bedroom to the bathroom. The double door means that less space is taken up when opened and the full height allows for ease of installation of a ceiling mounted hoist, if required. A level access shower tray has been installed rather than sloping the floor to a floor drain because a shower tray is a familiar object found in most homes, sloping floors are not. The bathroom walls are tiled but this is relieved by a feature band of colour tiles with motifs. Handrails have a contrasting band but the white sanitaryware does not contrast with the background walls. Bathroom wall areas that are not tiled are a coloured paint to soften the overall feel.

Residents provide their own carpeting to lounge and bedrooms but vinyl flooring is pre-installed to kitchen and bathroom.

The kitchen area opens directly off of the living room, to allow daylight into this area and allow views into the corridor from the living room (and vice versa). The kitchen cupboards and fittings are all of a familiar domestic appearance although the hob and oven are separate. Taps, cupboard door knobs, cooker controls are all of a familiar appearance. With the tenants here mostly being in the early stages of dementia this may not be an issue. There is a locked cupboard in the kitchen which contains cut-off switches. If there is a risk of a resident accidentally turning these off or not being safe using a hob, for example, then this cupboard can be locked, otherwise it is used by tenants for securing valuable items.

In the UK many people are more used to a ◄ cooker/hob/grill as one unit.

Kitchen worktops are generally of a flecked ◄ pattern in the surface and there are reports elsewhere of people with dementia perceiving these flecks as bread crumbs, and trying to brush them away.

Other dementia design features to these flats include movement sensors to flats, lockable radiator valves to prevent over or under heating; no sharp edges to furniture in communal areas, worktops, cupboards, etc; urine sealant on all floors.

Tenants own furniture goes a long way to giving each apartment its own identity, personality and a feeling of security when surrounded by familiar objects.

Rosewood Court does have its own secure entrance and staff/administration area which promotes a greater feeling of independence from Yew Tree Court or the day-care centre (Baytree Centre). These entrance doors are sliding and automatic (operated by electronic release). The sitting area by the entrance is not used much by tenants probably because there are no direct views outside and little direct daylight.

The corridors to Rosewood Court are not comfortable spaces. As stated above the kitchen windows looking into the corridors are liked by residents but the shelf recess (originally intended for milk carton delivery) for does not appear to have been used fully for personalising each door area. Most kitchen windows however have small displays of flowers or ornaments in them. By placing a small table and chairs at these ends there is an 'event' with views outside. To Yew Tree Court the door recess is larger creating the feel of a porch and there is also a contrast in the carpet (which could be problematic for dementia) Light sensors allow a recessed downlighter to come on above the apartment door when someone is stood by the apartment door.

> At 1.5metre width corridors are the minimum width possible and there is no variation to the space or finishes to break it up visually.

> The lay-in grid suspended ceiling is necessary for access to services but the uniformity of level adds to the apparent length of the corridor. The height of the ceiling also feels uncomfortably low. To the ground floor the corridors open out into the garden areas but to the first floor there is, in effect, a dead-end.

The handrails contrast with the walls and the wall/floor junctions are clearly defined. Each front door is a different colour and looks like a front door to a house, with a letterbox and two door viewers, one at standing level and one at wheelchair level. The ground and first floor have a different colour scheme to walls, carpets and handrails to help with orientation. Communal toilet doors are all coloured red and have raised wording, a raised symbol and writing in braille in contrasting colour for multiple cues.

A communal lounge/dining area is provided to each floor but only the ground floor area is used daily. There are glazed panels allowing views in and out from passing activity in the corridor and this also allows some borrowed daylight into the corridor. This is overcome to a degree by locating the kitchenette area and dining area here, which are 'inward looking' activities with the lounge sitting area by the windows, where tenants can look out or have more daylight for reading.

> This space suffers from being located in an internal corner of the building which minimises the amount of natural daylight and views out that can be used.

Whilst the ceiling is of a non-institutional plain plasterboard there is **no variation in its level to help differentiate spaces.** Recessed downlights, hanging pendant light and wall lights allow for a variation in lighting to suit moods or activities. The kitchenette is intended for making drinks and snacks only, and the fixtures and fittings are all of a familiar appearance. Meals can be served to a tenant or group of tenants here if they wish, the meals being brought from the main kitchen.

The Rosewood garden faces south to maximize daylight all day. Access from the lounge is located at the internal corner of the building. This can be because of having to walk a distance and then to be 'in the open'. Many people with dementia feel more secure when sitting with their back to or near a wall. There is access from the ends of the bedroom corridors and a pathway linking the two corridor ends and back to the lounge avoids any dead-end situations on the ground floor.

> Proximity to an adjoining bedroom window restricts the area of patio space directly in front of the lounge. Therefore to sit outside a tenant has to make their way to the central paved area which may deter some.

The central seating area has raised planting beds which tenants use and the paving is of brick and concrete flags with the walking paths of tarmacadam. There have been no reports of these contrasting surfaces being a problem; again this could be because of the tenants here only being in the early stages of dementia. Seating, a bird table and small ornaments also provide activity for the garden. The edges of the garden slope down to the site boundary and these have been planted with a variety of shrubs. There are steel fence railings to the slope to overcome any dangers of a steeply sloping surface. There are also security issues with local youths which these railings help to address.

Rosewood Court provides an environment where people, either as individuals or couples, with the early stages of dementia can be accommodated in a safe and secure environment whilst still maintaining their own independence and lifestyle. Providing opportunities for social contact is key to MHA philosophy and the provision of communal lounges and garden and the kitchen windows allows the opportunities for this to happen, overcoming the potential problem of people staying in their apartment and not coming out. This type of extra-care accommodation for people with dementia is likely to become more popular in the UK in years to come.

Sunrise of Vancouver

REASONS FOR SELECTION

➤ Relaxed homelike atmosphere

➤ Variety in room layouts, including apartment accommodation

➤ Residents with dementia live on upper floors

➤ Flexibility in activities and mealtimes

➤ While households of 31 residents are very large and against accepted practice, there are useful design features here worthy of consideration

SUNRISE OF VANCOUVER
999 West 57th Avenue
Vancouver
British Columbia V6P 6Y9
Canada

Contact for further information
Damien McGoldrick, Executive Director
vancouver.ed@sunriseseniorliving.com

Owner Sunrise Senior Living

Website www.sunriseseniorliving.ca

External appearance is of an apartment building, nothing to indicate any special needs of the residents. Changes in materials and projecting bays reduce the apparent height of the building

Open since
August 2003

Architect
C.E.I. Architects, Vancouver

Resident profile
75 residents who require assisted living.
31 residents with dementia (Sunrise use the word 'reminiscence').
There is a large Chinese community in Vancouver and there are several residents of Chinese descent at this home.

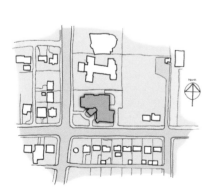

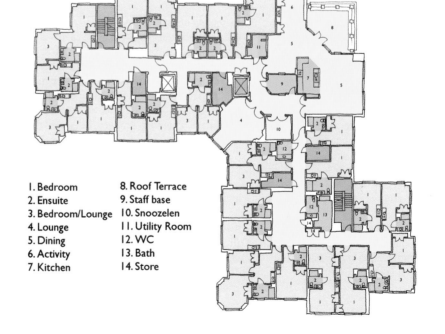

1. Bedroom
2. Ensuite
3. Bedroom/Lounge
4. Lounge
5. Dining
6. Activity
7. Kitchen
8. Roof Terrace
9. Staff base
10. Snoozelen
11. Utility Room
12. WC
13. Bath
14. Store

Number of residents
16 residents who require assisted living to Ground floor
31 residents who require assisted living to First Floor
31 residents with dementia residents on Second floor
31 residents who require assisted living to Third Floor
106 residents total

Typical bedroom floor area
There are several different bedroom types (areas include en-suite)
Type 210 - 25.7sq.m; Type 202 – 28.0sq.m; Type 111 – 30.0sq.m;
Type 216 – 36.4sq.m; Type 206 – 38.0sq.m; Type 226 – 38.7sq.m (double room)
Type 222 – 45.0sq.m (double room); Type 204 – 56.0sq.m (double room)

Floor area of each household
1750sq.m

Building density
60sq.m per resident (people with dementia)
56sq.m per resident (assisted living)

Site area
5890sq.m

Site density
55.0sq.m per resident

Staffing
Eight management staff
100 care staff in total
Kitchen staff, housekeeper, maintenance and activities

Service and ancillary space
On the ground floor are the main kitchen and dining areas for the residents requiring assisted living and the main laundry is in the basement for linen, with each floor having its own utility/laundry room. Deliveries are via the basement, accessed from the rear.

To the reminiscence household all meals are prepared in the main kitchen and brought to the smaller kitchen in the household.

Meals and laundry
Whilst meals are prepared in the main kitchen and brought to the reminiscence household, the food can be kept warm allowing the resident to eat when they want to, not at a fixed meal time.

Recreational cooking can also be undertaken in the kitchen within each household but this is limited to tea/coffee, snacks and food that can be cooked in a microwave.

Residents can do their own personal laundry within each household; linen is taken to the main laundry in the basement.

Activity area is in the foreground with dining and open-plan kitchen beyond. Kitchen area acts as a focus for the space and a lowered ceiling helps to define this and relieve the large expanse of ceiling. **Reflections on the polished floor surfaces could be perceived as being water on the floor.** Square window to the right is from the staff base allowing for discreet monitoring. Domestic furniture, tablecloths, curtains and wall pictures add to the homely feel.

Sitting area by bedroom doors: Different sitting areas have different themes with pictures and ornaments on the theme which help residents identify their own areas. Size and proportion of the space, change of ceiling levels, familiar looking furniture styles, carpet, light fittings, dado rail, and ceiling coving create a warm and cosy space. Variety in lighting can also be achieved here with ceiling lights, wallights and table lamps. However **there is no natural daylight** – apart from the top floor which can utilise rooflights

Site context

Suburban corner plot on a busy road in South Vancouver serving the residential areas of Sahunessy, Kerridale and Point Gray. There are several protected trees at the corner of the site.

Philosophy of care

Mission: To champion quality of life for all seniors
Principles of Service: Encouraging independence; Enabling choice; Preserving dignity; Celebrating individuality; Nurturing the spirit; Involving family and friends;
Core Values: Passion; Joy in Service; Stewardship; Respect; Trust; Foundation;
Belief in the sacred value of human life
This is displayed in wall-mounted frames throughout the home and on business cards.

Philosophy expression in the building design

The main focus is to make the whole building and each household feel like a welcoming, comfortable home. There are several intimate lounges, alcoves, craft areas, verandas and sunrooms to allow quiet or busy activities to take place. There are also roof terraces and a sensory garden.

Every room has an en-suite shower-room and there are therapeutic spa baths on each floor Long empty corridors are avoided and there is bright, yet soft, lighting.

Aspects of the building design that work well and which are worth repeating?
- *The corridors end in a sitting area and each area has a different theme*
- *Different room types add individuality and give flexibility of choice for residents and their families*
- *Double rooms allow for couples to live together, and can be arranged as two bedrooms or a bedroom and lounge*
- *Entrance areas are inviting and there are subtle sensory touches such as free popcorn, background music, the presence of a concierge, not a receptionist. (Background music could be confusing to someone with dementia. There is no background music to the dementia household in this building)*
- *The central staff base allows residents to come in and sit with the staff and personal conversations or meetings can take place here*
- *Families and visitors comment positively on the building and the atmosphere generated.*

Other comments
- *The ground floor sensory garden is tucked away at the rear of the building and is underused*
- *Traffic noise is a problem at the front of the building, roof terraces at the rear overcome this*
- *Lift opening out into the common areas is a problem for residents with dementia getting into the lift unsupervised*
- *Whilst there is an activity schedule in the reminiscence area, apart from key activities such as music therapy, this is a guideline only. Staff go with the mood and wishes of the residents and allow them to create their own daily routines*
- *The multi-sensory room is little used for its original intention. If a resident needs to be calmed down, they are more likely to be taken back to their room, which is a familiar environment with familiar objects.*

Outdoor roof terrace: Roof overhang, full-height trellis screen with glass and overhanging pergola, whilst providing a secure area enclose the space to an extent that **it does not feel like an outdoor space**.

• *The roof terrace does not feel like an external space because of overhang from above and extensive guarding.*

AUTHOR'S COMMENT

Households of 31 residents are much larger than other household sizes featured in this book and is against the international consensus on smaller, family sized, households. However there are interesting design aspects here that are worth looking at.

The Sunrise homes use generic floor layout plans that are adapted as required to suit each particular site. The entrance areas with double-height spaces, grand staircases and lounge, dining and veranda areas leading off feels like entering a large mansion. The external appearance is reduced in scale with mixed materials and projecting and recessed bays.

The central common areas are an interesting sequence of rooms and each space has an intimate feel to it although they are all open-plan. The open plan allows residents to orientate themselves and see where they are as well as allowing staff to monitor the residents discreetly.

Separating the activity and dining areas works well and avoids problems of residents confusing doing an activity in an area, or at a table, they would normally eat from. Staff find that most residents spend their time in these areas, rather than the lounge because of the activity and ability to watch the daily life of the household going on around them.

The sitting areas at the end of each corridor avoid any dead ends although they suffer from a lack of natural daylight, except for the top floor. Each sitting area has a different theme and this adds interest and helps with orientation. Objects rather than colours are used to help orientation – for example, a theme of 'movies' might have framed Hollywood movie posters from the 1940s, a director's style chair and a traditional conical megaphone.

There is a large Chinese community in Vancouver and there are several residents of Chinese descent at this home. Traditional-looking oriental vases, mah-jong sets, and paintings are all familiar objects to these people and strategic placing of these can act as orientation devices for them. Some of these residents who speak Chinese as their first language revert back to this in conversation. This can cause communication difficulties.

Some of the room layouts are odd with a long narrow hallway, or a large space by the door, with no natural daylight, but overall floor areas are very generous in the bedrooms. The double rooms provide what are essentially, self contained flats to each floor which allows couples to live together or, for example, two sisters.

The variety of rooms also helps with orientation, and gives a personal identity to each resident. A resident could visit a neighbour in another room, which, if this is a different layout, would be like going out to visit a neighbours apartment in an apartment block.

Wall paintings, drop lighting, workbench, dolls house and other familiar objects give a domestic and homely atmosphere to this property. The toy workbench and dolls were originally provided for visiting grandchildren to play with but residents use them too.

Overall the building is homely, welcoming and comfortable and aims to be true to the Sunrise Homes mission to 'champion the quality of life for all seniors'. It is also interesting to note that throughout the Sunrise organisation the word 'dementia' is replaced with the word 'reminiscence'.

Entrance hall: Impression is of the entrance to a mansion house. Concierge is at a desk with mission statement framed on wall behind. Communal spaces on either side of the entrance and behind open up the ground floor as semi-public areas with upper floors as private areas.

Staff base is in the room to the left with windows allowing views in and out. Dining room is through the opening. **Change from carpet to polished floor is very strong and could be perceived as a step by some people.** Desk, chair and wall light are familiar looking objects and people often sit here. **Unfortunately there is no direct daylight into this space.**

Terrace Gardens

REASONS FOR SELECTION

➤ **Dementia design principles applied to a tropical environment**

➤ **Each household is three buildings**

➤ **Verandas used as extensions to the rooms**

➤ **Residents include people from the indigenous community**

TERRACE GARDENS
1 Kettle Street
Farrar, Palmerston
Northern Territory NT 0832
Australia

Contact for further information
Rosemary Jeffery, Director of Nursing
don.terrace.gardens@bigpond.com

Owner Frontier Services

Website www.frontierservice.org

External appearance is of several tropical houses. This reduces the overall scale of the development and allows a cooling breeze around the buildings.

Open since
December 2001

Architect
KLCK Woodhead International

Resident profile
42 of the residents have dementia and half of these are physically frail as well. 14 of the residents have physical disabilities. At the time of writing there are ten residents of Aboriginal background.

Number of residents
Three groups of 12 residents.
One group of 20 residents.
56 residents in total plus two respite care.

Each group household consists of three buildings; two sleeping blocks and a communal room block. There is a staff building shared between every two households.

North

1. Bedroom
2. Ensuite
3. Lounge
4. Dining
5. Kitchen
6. Store
7. Corridor
8. Veranda
9. Covered Walkway

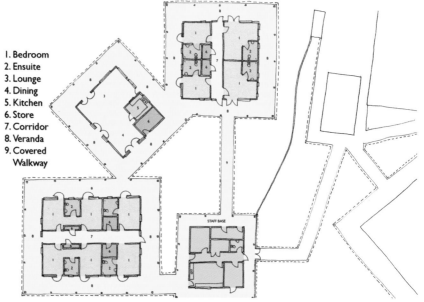

STAFF BASE

Typical bedroom floor area

Single bedroom 17.5sq.m plus 6.0sq.m en-suite: 23.5sq.m total
Double bedroom 24.25sq.m plus 6.0sq.m en-suite: 30.25sq.m
There are 8 double rooms, 12 single rooms with private en-suite, 28 single rooms with shared en-suites.

Floor area of each household

200sq.m sleeping block 1
273sq.m sleeping block 2
143sq.m communal block
Total: 616sq.m

Building density

51.3sq.m/ resident

Site area

17,487sq.m

Site density

301.5sq.m/ resident

Staffing

In total there are:
Three management staff
20 registered/enrolled nurses
40 care assistants
10 ancillary staff
During the day there are nine care staff (four are nurses), four team leaders, two activity staff and six ancillary staff. Overnight there are two registered nurses and eight care staff.

Service and ancillary space

Each household has a central block with its own kitchen. There is a central kitchen, laundry and administration block which is linked to each household via covered, ramped walkways. There is also an activity room which is used as a respite day room and is also the designated cyclone shelter.

Meals and laundry

There is a central kitchen where lunch and dinner are prepared and served at set times, which can be varied if required. Breakfast, drinks and snacks are prepared within the small kitchen adjacent to the lounge/dining area with no set times. Generally residents are not involved in meal preparation.

There is a central laundry where all the laundry is done.

Veranda: Didgeridoo and wall paintings are familiar objects for the residents of Aboriginal origin. And help them to identify their own households. Some residents prefer to sleep outside on the veranda.

Veranda: This extends around all four sides of each building. Each block has a different colour (see introduction) and surface finish (e.g. profiled metal cladding) to help residents identify their own sleeping block or the lounge/dining block. Concrete floor surfaces are cool to touch. Bedroom buildings have a central corridor 'breezeway.'

Site context
Sloping site on the outskirts of a small town south of Darwin and adjoining a health precinct.

Philosophy of care
To provide the best care to all individuals who live and work at Terrace Gardens, through a peaceful, harmonious, respectful and homelike environment. Staff promote and encourage family contacts, friendship and community links.

Philosophy expression in the building design
Residents are allowed to be independent whilst providing onsite access to professional services. Large verandas surrounding each building allow for quiet as well as active areas Each building has a homelike, domestic appearance typical of tropical houses. Overall the site has the atmosphere of a resort, set amongst lush tropical gardens. Large rooms allow residents' own furniture to be brought in, the hospital bed is the only institutional type of object. Staff uniforms are not compulsory.

Are there any aspects of the building design that work well and are worth repeating?
- *The size and layout of the bedrooms and en-suites works well, as do the shared en-suites*
- *Households of 12 residents are a good size and also work well*
- *The administration block being detached from the housing reduces any institutional overtones*
- *Verandas surrounding each block allow for residents choice in sitting or activities but present a problem with monitoring by staff.*

Other comments
- *Verandas on all four sides of each building creates problems for staff in monitoring residents*
- *There are long travel distances, and therefore time, for staff to move about the development which is inefficient.*

AUTHOR'S COMMENT
This building is unique when compared with the others featured in this publication in that the design is very much an application of the principles of dementia design to a tropical environment.

Each household is four buildings consisting of two sleeping blocks, lounge/dining/kitchen block with a nurse building shared between two households. The lounge/dining/kitchen block is air-conditioned but the sleeping areas are naturally ventilated.

The buildings have the appearance of several tropical houses in a resort-like environment, not one large building, thus creating a more domestic scale.

With the buildings spread across the site this also creates opportunities for breezes to flow through the building and to maximize natural ventilation rather than relying on air conditioning for cooling.

There are visual cues in the colour of the walls (see introduction), privacy is provided for by the verandas and different views are also achieved – inward to the gardens or outward to the

While the implications of this were discussed ◄ during the design of the building, staff find monitoring of residents difficult with the layout of the buildings and inefficient in terms of travel distances.

road, residents can choose for themselves. Hanging objects and different patterns on external sunblinds also help with cueing. Some of the objects are digeridoos, boomerangs and other items familiar to the residents of Aboriginal background.

Each bedroom has access to the veranda and to a corridor running down the centre of each block. Cross-ventilation is provided at high and low level by louvers with the corridor acting as a 'breezeway'.

Overhanging verandas, ceiling mounted fans, cladding and hard floor surfaces also keep the premises cool. Each veranda has a handrail and garden to separate it from the garden areas so a degree of discreet control is maintained. There are locked gates to the walkways separating each household and the central service buildings.

'Clutter' can be perceived as oppressive in the tropical heat, clean lines and surfaces being preferred. Carpets would soon harbour mould and mites. Tiling and sealed or painted concrete are preferred and are cool to the touch. Walls appear bare for this reason.

There are 10 residents of indigenous origin at Terrace Gardens. Often these residents will sleep outside on the veranda. There are large cultural differences in their needs; Aboriginal Australians brought up in an urban environment have a different outlook from those brought up in a rural environment, e.g. rural Aboriginal people have no concept of possessions and some residents arrive with little more than the clothes on their backs.

On top of this are issues with different clans and alcohol issues. Double bedrooms are popular with Aboriginal residents. Sleeping together as a family and sleeping outside is a familiar lifestyle for these residents.

Terrace Gardens is an excellent example of demonstrating how the principles of dementia design can be adapted and applied to any context. Whilst most of the built features of Terrace Gardens would not be appropriate for a temperate climate, the principles of the design and the thought behind the application of those principles is the key.

Communal building: This is shared between two bedroom buildings. Only this building is air-conditioned. Tiled floor surfaces are cool to touch and typical of tropical houses.

Covered walkways and tropical garden areas between buildings. The slope of the site requires walkways to be ramped. A continuous handrail around walkways and verandas deters residents from walking out of the shade (or into the rain during the wet season) or over landscaped areas, but without giving the impression of being enclosed.

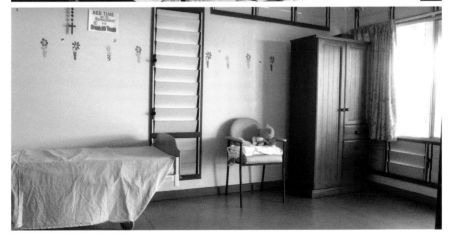

Bedroom: Louvers at high and low level provide natural cross-ventilation. Clean lines and minimal clutter and decoration are preferred in tropical areas, otherwise the impression is 'oppressive.' Rural indigenous people have a different concept of possession to other cultures and may arrive with little more than the clothes on their back.

Conclusion

BIBLIOGRAPHY

The following publications were consulted but this should not be considered to be an exhaustive or definitive list of publications. Such a list can be obtained from the Dementia Services Development Centre (DSDC) at the University of Stirling, Scotland. (www.dementia.stir.ac.uk)

American Institute of Architects (2004) *Design for Aging Review*, Mulgrave: Images Publishing Group.

Calkins M.P. (1988) *Design for Dementia: Planning Environments for the Elderly and Confused*, Maryland: National Health Publishing.

Judd S., Marshall M., Phippen P. (1998) *Design for Dementia*, London: Hawker Publications

Just Another Disability (1999) *Making Design Dementia Friendly* (information sheets), University of Stirling: Dementia Services Development Centre

Just Another Disability (2002) *Tools for the Future: A Strategic Brief and Audit Tool for Houses and Flats for People with Dementia*, University of Stirling: Dementia Services Development Centre

Just Another Disability (2002) *Tools for the Future: A Strategic Brief and Audit Tool for Buildings where People with Dementia Live as a Group Supported by Staff*, University of Stirling: Dementia Services Development Centre

Kotilainen H., Virkola C., Eloniemi-Sulkava U., Topo P. (2003) *Dementiakoti*, Helsinki: Suomen Dementiahoitoyhdistys Ry

Manthorp C. (2005) 'Growing Old Graciously', article in *The Guardian* newspaper: 9 November 2005

Pollock A. (2001) *Designing Gardens for People with Dementia*, University of Stirling: Dementia Services Development Centre

Pollock R. (2003) *Designing Interiors for People with Dementia*, University of Stirling: Dementia Services Development Centre

Pollock R. (2006) *Designing Lighting for People with Dementia*, University of Stirling: Dementia Services Development Centre

Regnier V. (2002) *Design for Assisted Living*, New York: John Wiley and Sons

Wijk H. (2001) *Colour Perception in Old Age*, Gothenburg: Department of Geriatric medicine, Gothenburg University

There is an international consensus on the effects, perception and how the surrounding environment can affect people with dementia. The facilities featured in this publication have all taken on board these principles and adapted them for each particular context, culture and within local regulations.

In an ideal world every facility would incorporate all the features mentioned, but in reality there are constraints of cost, time, location, regulations and so on which will inevitably affect the final built form.

The built environment is just one aspect of a total person-centred care approach. The approach, attitude and the delivery of care is equally or more important. The design and layout of buildings should allow, facilitate and add to the quality of care and to the quality of life of the residents, their families and the people who provide care for them.

This publication has provided examples that illustrate the principles of dementia design, as explained in the introduction:

Design should compensate for disability

Examples of where the design has compensated for someone with impaired memory can be seen where an open plan arrangement provides high levels of visual access allowing bedrooms, kitchen and other rooms to be seen from communal areas. Many designs illustrated also avoid any 'dead-end' situations so a resident can always return to their starting point.

Compensating for impaired reasoning is demonstrated by contrasts between walls, floors and junctions, contrasts between furniture upholstery and floors, contrasts between sanitary ware, toilet seats, grab rails and wall tiling. Similar floor tones avoid a perceived 'step' by having too marked a contrast. Tactile materials can be used to alert someone to a change in direction or end of a handrail.

Compensating for impaired learning is illustrated by the multiple cues for doors, such as all toilet doors being a single bright contrasting colour with a picture as well as words. Objects or architectural features work better than colour for orientation. An entrance wall can be curved, for example, or have a noticeably different texture such as concrete. Motifs on doors or at eye level on walls and noticeably different joinery can give an identity to each household and cues for residents to know where they are.

It is interesting that generally the Dutch approach is to eschew many of these cues and orientation with the viewpoint that these would not be used in your own home. This extends to not having en-suite toilets as these are not common in Dutch houses. However, their approach of having households of six residents and for each household to operate as a self-contained family unit does create a more domestic lifestyle for the residents. Anecdotal evidence suggests a reduced level of stress in residents here compared to traditional nursing homes. Stress can also be shown to be reduced by having quiet alcoves and spaces.

Design should maximise independence

This has worked with success where a resident can safely explore or walk around the household making their own choices. Scandinavian examples incorporate this internally because of the long and severe winters. Australian examples use the outdoor spaces, making the best use of the climate.

Design should enhance self-esteem and confidence

Lowered kitchen work surfaces and a kitchen layout enabling staff not to face a wall when in the kitchen allow residents to sit and get involved with kitchen activities. The option for residents to contribute to the running of the household by peeling vegetables or similar everyday tasks is important in maintaining a continuation of their everyday life. Providing a kitchenette within a resident's own personal space allows them to make a drink or snack independently and not have to go to the kitchen, where other activity may be taking place.

Design should demonstrate care for staff

A separate staff lounge is provided in most places, separate from the staff base or study within each household. Separate meeting rooms, training rooms, management offices and spaces for private meetings with residents' families allow staff to take a break from sometimes stressful situations.

Design should be orientating and understandable

Familiar-size spaces, objects and fixtures and finishes are essential. Domestic-scale rooms, homely-looking furniture, potted plants, ornaments, domestic kitchen cupboards, cross-head separate hot and cold water taps are all examples of objects familiar to people. This is very much influenced by culture and context. Shiny floors are common in Scandinavia and reflections are familiar to someone having seen such reflections in their own homes all their lives. In the UK floors tend to have a carpet finish and reflections on a shiny floor would be perceived as being wet.

Design should reinforce personal identity

Rooms large enough to have residents' own furniture and personal possessions is essential. The option of having residents' furniture in communal areas can also work successfully. Memory boxes allow for personalising a door area as well as providing a cue for a resident to identify their own room and telling others about the person whose room that is. Family-sized households also allow individual personalities to shine through.

Design should welcome relatives and the local community

The examples illustrated do not look institutional, be it the appearance of a hotel, apartment block or bungalow; contemporary or traditional design; and they are located in residential areas. The ability for residents to watch the world going by outside, to visit the local shops or for the local community to come in, such as students from a local art college to do craft activities with residents, all integrate the residents within the neighbourhood and eliminate any notion of isolation or being institutionalised.

Design should allow control of stimuli

Providing 'hidden' kitchens behind visible kitchens where noisy kitchen activities can take place and use of sound absorbing finishes, such as carpets, can cut down on distracting background noise. Doors fitted with closers that do not slam closed are also ideal, especially if the closer can be hidden from view. High levels of lighting are essential for people with poor eyesight but this needs to be controlled. External sunblinds can control bright daylight and the consequential glare and harsh shadows which can cause confusion. A central courtyard space or communal areas with windows on both sides can provide natural cross-ventilation. There is a conflict with most Building Regulations which aim to remove all smells from inside buildings. Cooking smells are desirable for their subtle stimulation; other smells are not so desirable and need to be removed. Careful design is required.

There are several key issues on specific matters that arise from the built examples illustrated:

Familiar environment

Creating a homely, domestic, home-from-home feel to the interior and exterior spaces is essential. Of course different people from different backgrounds and different cultures have different ideas on what constitutes 'home.' A tropical house, contemporary apartment block and traditional bungalow are all illustrated here; are all very different building types and each would be a familiar 'home' in their own way to people from different backgrounds. It is the size, scale and proportion of spaces that is the key to a domestic and familiar space.

Furniture, fixtures and fittings should also be familiar. It is generally accepted that spatial sense develops between the ages of 15 to 25 years, so someone with dementia who is 80 years old in 2006 will more easily understand a built environment similar to that from the years 1941-1951. The 'front room' or 'parlour', separate hot and cold water taps, hinged doors are all examples of familiar spaces, fixtures and fittings room to this generation. It is interesting to see that where contemporary interiors and contemporary furniture have been provided, residents' own furniture is more traditional. In the future, people who will be living in these buildings will have grown up in the 1950s and 1960s and their perceptions and expectations will be different.

Size of households

The Dutch facilities illustrated favour households of six residents as this is the size of a large family and this concept extends through the design and care to make things as they would be in your own home, such as not having an en-suite. Most houses would normally have a bathroom across a hallway. Generally speaking, smaller households are better for people with dementia but there will be a need to compromise because of other factors such as funding regimes, staffing costs, and regulations. It would appear that households of between 11-13 residents is often seen as cost effective.

Communal spaces

The arrangement of communal rooms and spaces can vary. Separate rooms are more familiar to people who have grown up in houses with a separate kitchen, living room and front room. However, open plan living is becoming more familiar to people now and there are advantages of this in terms of helping people with impaired memory. It would seem important though to have a separate activity space; there are comments from staff that residents get confused if they associate sitting at a certain place to eat, only to find they are about to do something else. It is also interesting to note that where a kitchen/dining area and a separate lounge have been provided, residents seem to prefer to spend their time in the kitchen/dining area where all the activity is. Views out from communal areas to the world outside avoid any feelings of isolation or being 'institutionalised'.

Traditionally the 'front room' or 'parlour' used to be where people had their best furniture and entertained visitors to their house. Providing this type of semi-formal space and fitting it out to look like a 'front room' is a recognisable space for many people and where these have been built they seem to be used for entertaining visitors as well as a quiet space or informal meeting room.

As previously explained, it is important to provide the spaces for residents to be able to walk about and make their own choices as to where they want to be in the household. Some of the examples illustrated have incorporated a looped path which is a series of events – sitting areas, corner windows, verandas, etc. so residents can safely move around according to their own moods and choices.

Bedroom size and en-suite

Bedroom size is influenced by cost factors and regulations. Current UK regulations require that bedrooms must have a minimum floor area of 12sq.m and be able to contain a specified list of furniture. 12sq.m should be considered as a minimum size as this is adequate as a bedroom only; in practical terms there is insufficient space for any other activity such as entertaining friends or relatives. However, there is an argument to say that bedrooms should be for sleeping only and other spaces are provided for communal activity, entertaining friends or relatives, etc.

Some Scandinavian bedrooms are more like studio apartments with space for a hallway, sitting and sleeping areas. Providing a small kitchenette reinforces a resident's independence, as mentioned above. These are often designed so that the water and electricity can be disconnected if required or the whole unit covered over or removed. It is also interesting to note the popularity of double bedrooms in Finland; double rooms are provided in other facilities but are for couples or two relatives and are in a small proportion compared to the number of single bedrooms in the same household.

For people with impaired memory a view of the wc from the bed can be important and doors that can be kept open are also critical to this. The layout of the en-suite is also important, if the first thing seen when walking in is a washbasin, some people may wash their hands and leave, forgetting they had meant to use the toilet. Space needs to be adequate for staff to help a resident if necessary but without the en-suite feeling too large and therefore uncomfortable. The toilet located in a corner, allowing staff either side may be a better arrangement than having the toilet in the middle of a wall. Mirrors can be perceived as windows by some people with dementia or their own reflection as a stranger in the room. Mirrors therefore should be capable of being removed if necessary.

Staff base

The phrase 'nurse station' has been deliberately avoided because of the institutional overtones. Staff do require a base from which to write reports, keep files and so on. A desk and cabinets that look like domestic fitted furniture, whether in the kitchen or lounge, and do not create a barrier between staff sitting at the desk and a resident, also gets away from any institutional feel. There can be issues with spills and general mess if the staff base is located in the kitchen. The Australians refer to the staff base as a 'study' as many houses would have a study which is a private space for doing work.

Outdoor spaces

Gardens and access to garden areas are an essential source of interest, activity and stimulation. Well-designed external spaces can become an additional communal space whether it is an enclosed garden, balcony or small patio with a view of activity and the outside world. Seats in the sun or shade; looped paths to walk along; the option of working at a raised planter or a greenhouse and take part in gardening activities; a variety of colour, textures and smells of plants and flowers; objects such as an old water pump, gazebo, fountain, flagpole, or bus-stop provide opportunities for discussion and to reminisce.

Colours and colour contrast

Colour perception tends to diminish with old age and relying on colour alone for orientation is really only effective for younger people with dementia. It is the colour contrast that can be more easily perceived and there are many examples illustrated of handrails, door handles, floor/wall junctions, toilets and washbasins that do exhibit good practice. There are also several examples that show bad practice and the annotation to the photographs highlights the bad practice as well as the good. It should be mentioned that a contrasting toilet seat is essential; relatively few places actually have this feature.

Flooring

As previously mentioned this is to a certain extent a cultural matter but an impervious sheet membrane such as a vinyl, linoleum or rubber floor tends to be a more common floor finish. There are practical reasons for this such as dealing with spills more easily than an absorbent carpet. Carpets are more common as a floor finish in the UK and products are available that are spill-resistant or carpet tiles which allow individual tiles to be removed. In countries where shiny floor surfaces are common everywhere, people are used to seeing reflections of windows and lights on the floor. Elsewhere, and certainly in the UK, these reflections would be perceived by some people as being wet, and therefore people would be reluctant to walk on this floor. Rugs can be seen in some examples; regulations in other countries would not allow rugs because of a potential trip hazard. Sharp changes in floor materials or colours are seen quite often although this can be perceived as a step by people with an impaired three-dimensional perception.

Ceilings

Lay-in grid suspended ceilings are not common in domestic architecture and is therefore an unfamiliar finish when used in a domestic environment. There are practical reasons for using this type of ceiling, mainly for access to services in the space above the suspended ceiling. In single storey buildings this should not be necessary because access to services can be through the attic space. Some places have used suspended ceilings throughout, others in circulation and/or communal spaces only. If practicalities require a suspended ceiling then they should be confined to circulation or activity areas, where people are less likely to be looking up at the ceiling. Plain-finish ceilings in bedrooms are domestic-looking and people will see the ceiling when in bed. An unbroken flat ceiling level can be monotonous over a large area. Varying ceiling heights and shapes and introducing recess spaces in the ceiling help to define spaces and introduce variety and stimulation.

Lighting

The ability to control natural daylight and to vary the artificial lighting is important. Glare and harsh shadows caused by bright sunlight can cause confusion and stress but too little light is a problem to people with impaired vision and can also make a space feel drab and gloomy. External sunblinds can reduce solar gain as well as providing shade. Curtains and pelmets are familiar to most people but can also restrict daylight coming in through a window. Ceiling lights, wall lights, downlighters and table lamps can all provide variety in lighting moods. Uplighters, particularly if set into a recessed ceiling space, can provide even glare free lighting. Hanging pendant lights and table lamps in lounge and dining areas are familiar objects; the style of lampshade and fitting is also important to consider for familiarity.

Doors

Sliding doors are to be found in everyday Scandinavian buildings and have been for some time. Hinged doors which are push or pull to open are more common in everyday life elsewhere. Sliding doors, therefore, whilst acceptable in Scandinavia because people are familiar with them may present problems elsewhere to people with dementia who might try to push or pull the door, thinking it is a traditional hinged door.

Personalising and providing multiple cues for residents to identify their own door can be seen in a variety of ways. Different colours may be more suitable for people without colour differentiation problems; different door panels may be too subtle for some others. Most bedroom doors have at least a number or nameplate. This in itself can be a cue especially if there is a picture or motif in the nameplate.

Front doors to households and staff-only doors have been dealt with in different ways. For some people with dementia the desire to explore can result in trying to open all doors and then there is frustration on finding a door locked. The ways of hiding doors vary from painting them the same colour of the walls to continuing wall finishes and handrails across the doors. The Australian way of having a separate external front door to each household for visitors reinforces the image of a domestic household.

Memory boxes

These have been used in several places and they take on different forms, from built-in display cabinets to a picture frame. As well as enabling a resident to identify their own room these also allow other people to know more about the person. Staff in many places often comment that they use the memory boxes to calm an agitated resident by talking to them about photographs or objects in the memory box.

It should also be noted that where memory boxes or other cues have not been provided, residents often fasten their own ornaments or names to their doors.

Multi-sensory rooms

These are sometimes called 'snoezelen' rooms and are relaxation/therapy rooms which aim to provide a multi-sensory experience through music, lighting effects, aromatherapy. They are sometimes combined with the assisted bathroom so water jets in the bath can add another stimulation. Generally, dedicated multi-sensory rooms are not used so much for this purpose and many places have a package of equipment that can be moved about to suit the residents' needs.

Staff roles

Not so much of a design matter as a management issue. The concept of staff carrying out multi-tasking roles i.e. cooking, cleaning, washing as well as providing care has been implemented in several different places. This is usually part of a general principle for each household to operate as a self-contained family unit and independently of the other households within the overall development. From a practical design viewpoint each household requires sufficiently large kitchen, utility room and store rooms but a central kitchen and laundry may not be required.

This is not an exhaustive list but an overview of the key issues that have arisen. The appendix to this publication is in the form of a checklist which can be used as a memory aid to ensure, as far as possible, that the principles of dementia design are incorporated into the design of new and refurbished buildings for people with dementia.

The future

Buildings designed and constructed today will be expected to have a life-span of at least 25 years, if not more. People who will live in these buildings in the future are sure to have a different outlook from the people who currently live in the accommodation illustrated. As previously explained, spatial awareness develops in most people between the ages of 15-25 years; future residents coming to live in the designs of today will have grown up in the 1950s and 1960s. Open plan living, car ownership, modern art, modern furniture, and pop music will be more familiar to them than to the current generation.

Culturally-appropriate dementia design is an issue which will become more relevant and important in the future.

People's expectations will also change in the future. Computers, mobile telephones, the internet, wireless technology, flat screen televisions, extra-care accommodation and perhaps a greater sense of independence are amongst the matters that future residents may expect to have as standard. The skill of designing for dementia today is to accommodate current demands and to design in the flexibility for change in the future as people's attitudes and expectations will inevitably change.

Appendix: Checklists

The following principles for the design of dementia-friendly buildings can be summarised in the form of the following checklist. This could be used as a memory aid to ensure, as far as possible, that the principles of dementia design are being incorporated into the design and specification of future care homes.

This list is a combination of the author's experiences and research carried out by others. Some publications of note are:
Designing Gardens for People with Dementia, by Annie Pollock (published by the University of Stirling: Dementia Services Development Centre: 2001)
Designing Interiors for People with Dementia, by Richard Pollock (published by the University of Stirling: Dementia Services Development Centre; 2003)
Designing Lighting for People with Dementia, by Richard Pollock (published by the University of Stirling: Dementia Services Development Centre; 2006)

This list is not exhaustive and is based on the homes visited and other literature on dementia design.

CHECKLIST OF FEATURES: ROOM BY ROOM

ENTRANCE AREAS
- Door monitor and/or CCTV so visitors can be seen
- Security – residents walking, unwanted visitors
- Residents cannot get out without staff knowing
- Level access
- Doors not too heavy to open
- Covered canopy over
- Remote from sleeping areas
- Access to garden areas

CORRIDORS/HALLWAYS
- Adequate width (wheelchairs and/or nursing beds, movable hoists)
- Street-like with variations in width
- Informal sitting areas/alcoves
- Display landmark objects to assist in cueing and orientation
- Familiar handrails
- No protrusions or trip hazards
- Clear route and signage/cueing to wc and assisted bath
- Sound insulation and privacy to bedrooms
- Personal recessed space in front of each bedroom door – lower ceiling with downlighter

COMMUNAL LOUNGE
- Adequate space – wheelchair manoeuvring
- Accommodate various activities without conflict
- Observe activities going on – inside and outside
- Contrasting scale of activities - personal spaces to group activities
- Domestic Scale, irregular shape, large rectangular rooms are institutional
- Domestic and familiar size, height and fittings – sofas, easy chairs, coffee tables
- Space for visitors
- Views out of windows when sitting
- Monitoring by staff

- Unobtrusive handrails
- Space for activity and homeworking activities
- Focal point e.g. TV
- Link to dining area
- Sound insulation to sleeping and other quiet areas
- Different furniture styles is a more domestic arrangement

COMMUNAL DINING
- This tends to be the time and place where all residents are together at the same time each day – therefore a focus for community spirit within each home
- Adequate space – wheelchair manoeuvring
- Domestic and familiar size, height and fittings
- Room for visitors
- Views out of window when sitting
- Monitoring by staff
- Unobtrusive handrails
- Proximity to kitchenette
- Sound insulation to sleeping and other quiet areas
- Several rectangular tables can be put together for greater flexibility
- Open sideboards encourage residents to participate in setting and clearing meals
- Avoid reverberation effects with noise of cutlery and crockery

KITCHENETTE
- Visible storage including fridge – glass fronted storage or no cupboard doors
- Utensils hang on butchers rail or blunt end hooks for better display/visibility
- Worktops to be contrasting colour to walls and floor
- Speckled worktop surfaces can be perceived as crumbs, so people with dementia may think they are not clean
- Ease of tea/coffee making
- Familiar recognisable fixtures and fittings
- Views out of window
- Cookers to have safety cut out or on/off control by staff
- Proximity to dining area and open for smells and sounds (cueing)
- Adequate lighting and ventilation
- Any cupboards off-limits to residents to have blank fronts
- See Fixtures and Fittings below for kitchen sinks and taps
- Hot cupboard allows flexibility in residents' meal times – institutional having set meal times and interrupting activities

BEDROOM
- Have variety of layouts between rooms as far as possible – helps recognition of individual rooms
- Impression of a flat/home/apartment, not a bedroom – have non-bedroom features
- Distinguish between sitting and sleeping areas
- Individuality of front doors
- Doorbell or knocker on each front door
- Visible storage
- Privacy
- Views out of windows when sitting
- View of wc from bed
- Pressure pads – resident security
- Domestic lighting, fixtures and fittings

- Surfaces for displaying personal artefacts
- Bed covers in coloured or muted pattern to contrast with carpet
- Front-facing wardrobes – today's clothes facing to the front
- Alternative bed layouts

EN-SUITE
- People with dementia need to see what they use
- Adequate ventilation
- Adequate non-glare lighting
- Low-level night-time lighting
- Shelving for toiletries, not cupboards
- Fully wheelchair-accessible
- Grab rails, sanitaryware, toilet seat, etc. to be contrasting colour
- Easy cleaning of surfaces
- Domestic feel – avoid all white tiling, which can look clinical
- Doors to be capable of opening outward – access in emergency
- Sliding doors can cause confusion –people try to push or pull open

STORAGE
- Day-to-day storage has to be seen and capable of use
- Secure storage to be hidden – door, architraves, and ironmongery to blend in with wall behind

CHECKLIST OF FEATURES: ELEMENTS

DOORS: EXTERNAL
- Secure both sides: Control of visitors to building and prevent residents from walking out
- Fire exit doors or other non-day-to-day use doors to blend into wall background (door colour, architrave same as wall surround)

DOORS: INTERNAL
- Colour code doors e.g. wc and bath doors all one colour, exit doors all one colour
- Bedroom doors to have scope for personalisation
- Bedroom doors to be a full door width plus a (usually fixed closed) half-width door for access of nursing beds, large furniture items
- Display cabinet for personal effects by door
- Picture of room contents fixed to door, e.g. bath
- Staff-access only doors to blend into background – door colour, architraves same as wall, continue skirting and handrails across door, no signage
- Highly visible emergency exit doors can be distracting

WINDOWS
- Cill heights allow view when sitting
- Capability for fitting of future automatic controls
- Trickle vents for background ventilation
- Reflections can cause confusion – consider position of light fittings

HANDRAILS
- Comfortable to touch
- Robust fixing – take full weight of a person
- Contrast to wall surfaces behind
- Visual and tactile indication that handrail is ending
- Raised tactile buttons can indicate features, e.g. 3 buttons indicates external door

SKIRTINGS, ARCHITRAVES, PICTURE RAILS
- Colour to contrast with and carpet to make clear distinction between wall/floor
- In wet areas coved skirting must contrast with floor
- Skirting on stairs to 'step' with the stairs along the wall

RAMPS
- Slip-resistant surface but suitable for someone shuffling
- Exposed edge to have distinctly visible kerb

STAIRS
- Main stairs to be visible and attractive
- Contrasting nosing
- Textured markers and colour contrasts in flooring to indicate presence of stairs
- Skirting on stairs to 'step' with the stairs along the wall

LIFTS
- Avoid mirror walls and ceilings or other highly-reflective surfaces
- Voice-over to announce landing levels
- Braille and tactile buttons to lift controls
- Service lift doors to blend in with walls behind so as to be hidden

STORAGE CUPBOARDS/ROOMS
- Storage areas which residents use to have open or glazed frontage
- Staff only cupboards/rooms to blend into wall background
- Ironmongery to be capable of supporting a person's weight

CHECKLIST OF FEATURES: FIXTURES & FITTINGS

BATHS AND TAPS
- Crosshead taps essential with blue/red and Hot/Cold indicators
- Baths to be standard domestic baths with portable hoists – parker/arjo baths and fixed hoists are institutional

SHOWER BASES AND CONTROLS
- En-suite floors to slope towards shower gulley
- Shower controls to be easy to see and operate

WC PANS, CISTERNS AND SEATS
- Seat to be contrasting colour to pan
- Sanitary ware and toilet roll holders to be contrasting colour to wall/floor finishes behind
- Traditional-looking sanitary ware required
- Contrasting colour lever handle or pull chain

WASHHANDBASINS AND TAPS
- Cross head taps essential with blue/red and hot/cold indicators
- Plug and chain preferred
- Sufficient space for soap, toothbrush, etc – holders to be contrasting colour to wall behind

DOOR HANDLES, LOCKS, KEYS, CLOSERS
- D type (return end) lever handles essential
- Large comfortable grip
- Small clearance at handle projection to avoid catching on sleeves
- Doorknobs should be avoided as they are very difficult to grip
- Contrasting colour/finish to door surface
- Window latches to be one-handed, single action locking and latching mechanisms
- Lock cases to have deep backsets to keep knuckles clear of doorstop checks
- Safety restrictors to windows essential, but quick release to upper floors to comply with Building Regulations
- Corridor and communal doors to be on hold-open door closers
- Ease of opening doors essential
- Traditional-looking letterboxes and baskets if required
- Numerals and nameplates can personalise bedroom doors – contrasting finish to door surface

HAT AND COAT HOOKS
- Large, easily visible, round edges
- Personal clothing hanging in view of door helps with room recognition

SHELVES
- Open display on shelves preferable to closed away in cupboards
- Shelving to contrast with wall for visibility
- High level shelving only for precious, fragile or irreplaceable items
- Staff-only items to be in cupboards

SIGNAGE
- Picture of room function or objects in them essential – e.g. picture of a toilet
- Lettering to be clear and large
- Contrast lettering/picture with background
- Colour code as doors, e.g. all bathroom, wc, etc the same colour
- Signs to be fixed to doors, not adjacent wall surfaces
- Fix slightly lower than eye level because people with dementia tend to look downwards
- Communal facilities could have shopfront types of signs, e.g. kiosk, hairdresser

CHECKLIST OF FEATURES: DECORATION, FURNITURE & FURNISHINGS

WALLS
- Wallpaper – strong patterns or images of real life objects should be avoided
- Colours to be muted but not dull, too bright causes confusion but colour differentiation fades with age
- Gloss paint causes reflections and confusion – silk finish better

FLOOR
- Contrasting floor colours and surfaces are perceived as a step
- Edges and steps to be clearly delineated – tactile surface in floor finish when near an edge
- Thresholds to be either invisible to encourage moving over them, or high contrast to deter movement of people into a room
- Carpets to allow for shuffling
- Carpet tiles preferable for cleaning and maintenance but no loose edges or joints
- Speckles in floor surfaces perceived as dirt or pebbles, which can cause anxiety in residents

TILES
- All-white tiling is very clinical
- Muted colours preferred
- Motifs in tiles of real-life objects to be avoided as they could be perceived as real objects by some people with dementia

CURTAINS/BLINDS
- Busy patterns to be avoided
- Contrast with main walls
- Curtains preferred to venetian or roller blinds

CHAIRS
- Comfortable and easy to sit down into and to stand up from
- Runners help with pushing/moving chairs on carpets, but may be too mobile on polished surfaces
- To be sturdy enough to support people when leaning on – cantilevered edges may tip up
- Variety of chairs in communal areas
- Upholstery to be contrasting to floors but no busy patterns or representations of real life objects

TABLES
- To be sturdy enough to support people when leaning on them because cantilevered edges may tip up
- Clear space for wheelchairs to sit at tables
- Rounded corners and edges
- Chairs with arms to be pushed under

BEDS
- Traditional-looking
- Ideally accessible from two sides but some people prefer one side only – fear of falling out
- Covers to contrast with floor but no busy patterns or representations of real life objects

WARDROBES
- Open front or clear front for display
- Partial open front can also display contents
- Robust, easy grip D handles in contrasting finish

LIGHT FITTINGS
- Traditional-looking essential
- Higher than normal lighting levels required but no glare and controllable to personal preferences
- Emergency lighting, etc to be discreet or incorporated into standard fittings
- Bedside lights to be touch-activated – switches are difficult to find in the dark
- Light shades allow for personal choices
- Dark corners to be avoided
- Strong shadows cast by lighting are perceived as a step or object

CLOCKS
- Analogue face clocks essential
- Luminous face for night-time visibility

MIRRORS, PICTURES, ORNAMENTS
- Mirrors can cause confusion, particularly full length mirrors, they can be perceived as another person
- Mirrors reflecting views out of windows cause confusion
- Pictures should be personal
- Low reflectance glass to picture frames
- Local lighting can highlight pictures as feature and aid orientation
- Ornaments help with memory and orientation
- Contact with personal objects/ornaments essential to residents

CHECKLIST OF FEATURES: SERVICES & UTILITIES

HEATING
- Underfloor heating can provide even distribution of heat and free up wallspace. However, difficult to control and problems with smells from spills and accidents
- Radiators to be low surface temperature, can be easily controlled but take up wall space and can lead to cold spots in a room

HOT/COLD WATER
- Scald control valves essential
- Automatic monitoring devices can prevent floods
- Overflow pipes to be situated to prevent external paths becoming wet or release of hot water onto anyone below
- See Baths and Taps above for taps

ELECTRICAL
- Contrast finish between switches, sockets and wall surfaces
- Switches, sockets not for use by residents to blend in with wall behind and tamperproof
- Dimple surface on switches gives tactile aid
- Neon indicators associated with 'on'

CHECKLIST OF FEATURES: EXTERNAL SPACES

- Open spaces have to be enclosed but in such a way that users are not drawn to the site edge
- Long vistas to be avoided
- Strong contrasts of light and shade are disorientating
- Choice of plants, trees, shrubs, etc. should avoid anything poisonous

PATIO
- Sheltered with sunny aspect
- Level hard surface
- Level access to building from communal areas
- Privacy to any bedrooms that overlook patio
- Space for activities e.g. bbq, potting plants, games, etc.
- Direct access to paths
- Moveable awnings, parasols, etc
- Planting beds against walls – some people will 'hug' the walls when outside

PATHS
- Should lead from and return to the patio area – walking path
- Have rest areas, see below
- Avoid abrupt changes of direction and dead ends
- Handrails required if steeper than 1in60 fall
- No fall greater than 1in20
- Different material/colour from patio or sitting areas to differentiate, but not so great to be perceived as a step
- Raised edges on planting beds
- Level access to grassed areas

PAVING MATERIALS
- Materials to be warm and domestic in colour and scale
- Trip hazards to be avoided – tarmac and brushed concrete avoid this but not very domestic. Coloured tarmac more appropriate
- Light-coloured or reflective materials can cause glare on sunny days
- Reflective materials also perceived as water
- Paviours appropriate for small areas
- Broken bond pattern for paving flags less likely to settle unevenly
- Highly-visible jointing pattern can aid direction-finding and movement
- Patterns in paving can encourage movement
- Gravel inappropriate for wheelchairs, Zimmer frames, shuffling. Use in areas where residents are discouraged to go
- Manhole covers, etc to have paving material set in. Blank covers perceived as a hole

RESTING & SITTING AREAS
- Ensure sufficient areas provided
- Enough space for bench and wheelchair not to impede path
- Degree of privacy required but not hidden – use trellis and low fencing
- Sheltered from sun and wind
- Have feature themes to each area e.g. bird table, planter, and sculpture
- Feature plants in these areas to provide stimulus

FENCE, WALLS, HEDGES
- Sometimes people with dementia try to climb over fences or walls
- No horizontal rails to fences that could be used as a ladder
- Boundary gates to be merged within fence design with concealed latches
- Gates for use by residents to be familiar-looking, self-closing, easy to see and easy-grip ironmongery
- Fences and walls to be appropriate to local environments – aids recognition and familiarity
- Planting against fence or wall will discourage people getting close to it
- Balconies to have perimeter planting to keep residents away from edge because of vertigo and the danger of trying to climb over

GARDEN FURNITURE
- Raised planters to avoid bending over but they are not always perceived as conventional flower and planting beds
- Pergolas provide 'gateways' from one area to another
- Seating to be solid, comfortable, with arms and capable of supporting weight of person
- Seating to have rounded edges
- Seating to be easy to sit down onto and easy to get up from
- Bird tables, pots, ornaments to be securely-fastened and capable of having a person leaning on them
- Avoid running water
- Objects and ornaments aid orientation and cueing
- Traditional objects, e.g. wheelbarrow, help with memory.